Divine Cookies

Tchipakkan

Divine Cookies

by
Tchipakkan

Hubbardston, Massachusetts

Asphodel Press
12 Simond Hill Road
Hubbardston, MA 01452

Divine Cookies
© 2005 Virginia Richards Taylor
ISBN 978-1-57433-777-8
Second Edition

All rights reserved.
No part of this book may be reproduced in any form
or by any means without the permission of the author.

Library of Congress Cataloging-in-Publication Data

Tchipakkan
Divine Cookies.
Summary:
A recipe book featuring cookies. A celebration of the world's best cookies and the gods and goddesses who inspire them.

[1. Cookbooks, recipes. 2. Mythology. 3. Cookies. 4. New Age.] 1. Title. [Non-Fic.]

Printed in cooperation with
Lulu Enterprises, Inc.
860 Aviation Parkway, Suite 300
Morrisville, NC 27560

*For Megan, who made this happen,
And for Claus, my favorite cookie taster.*

Acknowledgements:

*Thanks to Dan, Kat, and Willow
for always being there for me,
to Star for washing the same dishes
over and over again every half hour,
to Travis for showing up mysteriously,
to Bella, Raven, and Josh,
and to Aelfwine and all his squires,
and, of course,
to Ganesh, Thor, Freya and Mother Holle.
(Yeah, we got the dishes washed!)*

TABLE OF CONTENTS:

Introduction 1
The Great Mother 3
  Peanut Butter Donis
Inanna 5
  Inanna Stars
Ishtar 7
  Breasts of Ishtar
Cybele 9
  Attis Cookies
Yemaya 11
  Yemaya Cookies
Anansi 13
  Anansi Cookies
Loki 15
  Lokis
Hel 17
  Hel's Thumbprints
Odin 19
  Odin's Shields
Sleipnir 21
  Sleipnirs
Runes 23
  Rune Cookies
Frigga 25
  Frigga's Handmaidens
Mimir 27
  Mimir's Well Cookies
Fenris 29
  Fenris Bars
Tyr 31
  Tyr's Hands

DIVINE COOKIES

Freya 33
   Freya's Cookies
Frey 35
   Frey's Cakes
Thor 37
   Thor's Goats
Mjolnir 39
   Mjolnirs
The Norns 41
   Norn Cakes
Skadi 43
   Skadi's Skates
Mielikki 45
   Mielikki Bars
Bastet 47
   Bastets
Ra 49
   Ra Bars
Isis 51
   Isis Cakes
Osiris 53
   Osiris Puzzle Cookies
Hathor 55
   Hathor's Sistra
Bes 57
   Bes Cookies
Hermes 59
   Hermes' Coins
Janus 61
   Janus Cookies
Pan 63
   Pan Pipes
Aphrodite 65
   Aphrodite's Doves

Demeter..67
   Kores

Artemis..69
   Bows of Artemis

Hecate 71
   Hecate's Moons

Athena..73
   Athena's Owls

Amalthea 75
   Amalthea's Horns

Potnia 77
   Labrys Cookies

Gaea 79
   Gaeas

Bean Tighe 81
   Bean Tighe Stars

Brigit...83
   Brigit's Crosses

The Dagda 85
   Dagda's Club

The Morrigan.......................................87
   Death By Chocolate Brownies

Rhiannon..89
   Wafers of Rhiannon

The Celtic Tripple Goddesses 91
   Silver Wheels

Blodeuwedd 93
   Blodeuwedd's Flowers

Epona 95
   Epona's Horses

Herne..97
   Herne's Beasts

Beltane 99
   Beltane Flowers

The Green Man 101
    Green Man Nut Balls
The Green Man II 103
    No-Bake Green Men
Litha 105
    Litha Shells
Midsummer Night 107
    Titania's Lunettas
Asclepius 109
    Lammas Serpents
Lugh 111
    Lammas Crescents
Mabon 113
    Mabon Leaf Cookies
Samhain 115
    Tiny Samhain Stars
The Winter Lord 117
    Stags' Antlers
The Crone 119
    Crone Cakes
Yule 121
    Yule Wheels
Imbolc 123
    Imbolc Bites
Ostara 125
    Rabbit Ears
Lakshmi 127
    Sandalwood Print Cookies
Ganesha 129
    Ganesha's Treats
Kali 131
    Kali's Skulls
Kuan-Yin 133
    Kuan-Yin Bars

Amaterasu 135
   Amaterasu Rice Cookies
Pele 137
   Pele Shortbread
Coyote 139
   Coyote Snacks
White Buffalo Calf Woman 141
   White Buffalo Calf Woman Chips
Manitou 143
   Manitous
Corbie 145
   Corbie's Bribes
Chac 147
   Chac Mocha Snakes
Baba Yaga 149
   Baba Yagas
Strega Nona 151
   Strega Nonas
Witches' Hats 153
   Witches' Hats
Magic Wands 155
   Magic Wands
Index 157
Cookies Indexed by
Distinctive Ingredients 162

Introduction

I'm going to start off with the concept that you know how to make cookies already: that for most cookies, you cream the sugar into butter, then add the eggs, and sift the dry ingredients together before mixing them into the wet, or you rub the flour into the butter for a shortbread. or whip the sugar into the eggs for a meringue. This is a small book, and I don't have much space. Other cookbooks can give you more instruction if you need it.

Each recipe is paired with a story of a God, a Goddess or some other myth or legend that inspired the name or recipe. I am hoping that as you explore both the stories and the recipes that some of you will try a new cookie because you like the recipe, or you'll go out and learn more about some legend because you liked the cookie. (As I hope parents will enjoy sharing these myths and recipes with their children, I've given a "cleaned up" version of some myths. You'll find some of them more graphic if you look deeper. While I dislike altering traditional stories, I understand that sometimes it's better to learn them in stages, finding out more with age.)

In this one small volume. I've combined two of my passions: baking (and eating) cookies with the myths and legends of many lands. There are, of course, many more cookie recipes, and many, many more gods. So in theory, even when you've tried all of these, you can go on, and on, and on...

If you want more interesting cookie cutters, with everything from spiders to hippos, then check these Internet sites:

Pinocchio Productions: http://www.pinenose.com

Fusos: http://www.foosecookiecutters.com

The Cookie Cutter Shop: http://www.thecookiecuttershop.com

Sweet Celebrations: http://www.sweetc.com

Most of these recipes can be changed to be wheat-free by replacing the white flour with our Gluten Free Gourmet Flour. Make a batch by combining:

    1 cup tapioca flour
    2 cups potato starch
    6 cups rice flour

The Great Mother

The oldest representations of Goddess are Neolithic stone carvings of fat and/or pregnant women, known in later times as Magna Mater, the Great Mother. Several figurines, including the Venus of Willendorf, and the Laussel Venus, are small and possibly meant to be carried with the worshippers. The name Doni for the Great Mother comes from the Earth's Children series books by Jean Auel, which explores the lives of Neolithic people.

Peanut Butter Oonis

2 cup sugar
1 cup butter
1 tbsp molasses
2 eggs
1 cup peanut butter
1 tsp. vanilla
1 ¾ cup flour
1 cup whole wheat flour
1 ½ tsp. baking soda

Mix, roll into 4 sizes of balls. Form goddess figures by grouping two balls for the breasts, one smaller one for the head above and one larger one for the belly below. Add a pinch of dough for the arms and legs if wanted. Bake on ungreased sheets. (They do flatten a lot.)

time: 10-12 minutes
temp: 350°
yield: 3 dozen

INANNA

Inanna is the Mesopotamian Great Goddess, closely associated with Astarte and Ishtar, a goddess of love and war. She is also the Queen of Heaven, and her symbol is an eight-pointed star with a blue stone in the center.

Inanna, like Ishtar, descends to the underworld to visit her sister Ereshkigal, but she first warns her servant-maiden to tell the Sky God, Enki, if she does not soon return. She is made to leave her trappings of power at the seven gates to the Underworld. When she arrives, her grieving and angry sister has her hung on a hook to die, but as she is the goddess of fertility, the surface world starts to die with her. Enki intervenes and makes two sacred people out of clay to descend to the Underworld and save her; they gain her release by weeping in compassion for the grieving Ereshkigal. Inanna is allowed to return to the earth, but only if someone takes her place in the underworld. Ereshkigal's demons choose Inanna's consort, the shepherd king Dumuzi, thus creating the cycle of summer and winter.

Inanna's Stars

1½ cup sugar
3½ cups flour
1 cup butter
1 tsp. baking powder
1 egg
8 oz cream cheese
1 tsp. vanilla
½ tsp. almond extract
blueberry preserves

Mix everything but the preserves, chill, and roll out 1/8" thick. Try to find an eight-pointed star cutter, or use a four-pointed one, and cut out an even number of dough stars. Roll the stars slightly thinner, cutting a small window in half of them. Spread the cookies without holes with a thin layer of blueberry preserves, and stack the holed stars on top, sandwiching them. Bake on an ungreased sheet or baking parchment (especially if you use preserves).

time: 8-10 minutes
temp: 375°
yield: 90

ISHTAR

Ishtar was the major Babylonian Goddess, the Lady of fertility, love and war. Her sacred animals were lions, snakes and scorpions, and she was often shown holding forth her overflowing breasts to feed mankind. Like the similar goddess Inanna, the story of Ishtar's descent to the underworld is a common story of love and rebirth. Ishtar descended into the underworld in search of her slain love Tammuz. On the way down she had to pass the seven gates and leave one of her symbols of power at each: first her crown, second her lapis necklace, third her bracelets, her shoes at the fourth, her veil at the fifth, her robe at the sixth, and her last garment at the seventh, so she arrived in the underworld naked and powerless before her sister, Irkalla the queen of the underworld. There she died, but as the great god Shamash saw the world suffering from her absence, she was resurrected and returned. Tammuz represents the grain that is cut down at harvest, but is brought back to grow again by the fertile earth in the spring.

BREASTS OF ISHTAR

Dough:
- 2 cups white flour
- 1 cup semolina flour
- 1 cup butter
- 2 tbsp. water
- 1 tbsp. orange blossom water

Filling:
- 1 cup chopped walnuts
- ¼ cup sugar
- 1 tsp. orange blossom water
- 1 tsp. water
- (2 tbsp. powdered sugar)

Mix the flour and butter, moisten with the water and knead. Mix the filling. Form the dough into balls, make a dent in the middle and fill, then wrap the dough around it and seal well. Shape each cookie like a large gumdrop. Decorate tops and sides by pressing lines or dots in with a fork. Bake, dust with powdered sugar.

time: 20-22 minutes
temp: 400°
yield: 3 dozen

CYBELE

Cybele (pronounced Key-bel-le) was a Phrygian goddess whose cult spread to Rome where she was worshipped as another Magna Mater (Great Mother). She loved the mortal Attis who bled to death in a grove of pine trees. His blood dyed the violets red, and she kept his body preserved forever in a crystal or glass casket, as in the fairy tale Snow White.

Her priest/esses, the gallae, led a huge week-long celebration every March, washing the sacred stone of the cult, and carrying pine trees decorated with ribbons and flowers and images of Attis into the city. The Attis story is one of many myths of death and resurrection, and one of the most popular religions in Rome at the time of the coming of Christianity. Cybele wears a mural crown, which looks like the top of a castle wall, because when Attis was going to marry a mortal princess, she broke the city wall down with her head to stop the wedding. She is accompanied by lions, and holds a pine tree or branch. Attis is shown wearing a Phrygian cap with a little flap of cloth on the top.

A Tus Cookies

> 1 ¼ pounds of butter (5 sticks)
> 1 cup flour
> 1 cup sugar
> 1 teaspoon vanilla extract
> red (strawberry or raspberry) preserves

Blend the butter and sugar into the flour, and add the vanilla. Form the dough into finger-diameter rods and press a dent down the middle of each on an ungreased cookie sheet. (I use a chopstick and line the pans with baking parchment.) Bake for 15 minutes, then fill the impression with the preserves. You can pour it if you heat and stir it, but that's not necessary. Bake for another 10 minutes, until the bottoms just start to brown. While they are cooling, cut them into bite sized pieces.

time: 25 minutes
temp: 350°
yield: 5-6 dozen

YEMAYA

Yemaya is the Yoruba Great Mother, and the Orisha of the Sea and the Moon. Yoruba is an Afro-Caribbean religion where besides the One God, there are also many Orishas who are the personified aspects of nature and spirit. Orisha worship spread to the new world with the slave trade, and at that time the Orishas were identified with Catholic saints. It has since become the five religions known as Voudoun, Santeria, Candomble, Umbanda, and Palo Mayombe. Yemaya is the mother of many of the other Orishas. She has feast days on September 7th and New Years Day, where her followers set out food and candles on the beach to be washed away by the tides. She is associated with Mary as Star of the Sea. Her symbols are all sea creatures - pearls, shells, and sea birds. She's sometimes shown as a mermaid with a mirror and comb.

YEMAYA COOKIES

    1 cup powdered sugar
    ¾ cup butter
    8 oz. cream cheese
    2¼ cups flour
    ½ tsp. baking soda
    ½ tsp. mint extract
    green and or blue food coloring
    chocolate, melted in bowl over warm water

Cream sugar, cold butter, and cream cheese; mix in flour, soda, extract and food coloring. Divide the dough in two before using two colors. You can leave part of the dough white and layer all three colors then fold and mix- a little to make a swirled effect. Roll 1/8" thick and cut out with cutters shaped like fish, shells, ducks, etc. (If you are in a hurry, form dough into a roll, wrap and refrigerate dough, then slice and bake). Bake on ungreased sheets. When cool, drizzle with white chocolate (or dark - you can dot with white chocolate to look like pearls).

time: 10-12 minutes
temp: 325°
yield: 3 dozen

ANANSI

Anansi is an African trickster god, who is also popular in the Caribbean. Anansi was a very wise man. Wise things get repeated until they sound quite foolish, and Anansi was tired of his wisdom getting twisted. He gathered up all the wisdom in the world, put it into a calabash, and took it to the tallest tree in the world.

Anansi sometimes took his sons on his adventures, and his youngest son was traveling with him. "Wait here," Anansi said to his son, and he started to climb the tree, holding tight to the calabash, thinking that he would hide it in the branches so no one but he would mangle Wisdom ever again. It was difficult for a spider to climb as the calabash kept getting tangled in his legs. Down among the roots, Anansi's son watched him climb and fight with the bottle, and called up, "Father, what if you were to sling the bottle across your back?" Anansi stopped. Here was his youngest son, a child that had barely begun to think, and he had been more wise than Anansi! His son had shown him that wisdom must be shared, for if it is hoarded, it is worthless. He opened the calabash, and spread the wisdom over the world again, which is why today you can find wisdom anywhere, even in the mouths of idiots.

ANANSI COOKIES

This is an unusual savory biscuit, rather than a sweet one. Adults love them.

1 cups sugar	2 cups flour
½ cup butter	1 tsp. baking powder
1 egg	½ tsp. salt
3 tbsp brandy or	1 tsp. caraway seeds
1 tsp. brandy extract	

Mix the wet, then dry ingredients. Chill, then roll 1/4" thick, cut and bake. You can buy spider cookie cutters, and even spider-shaped sprinkles at Halloween, but if you don't have those you can make webs by (after baking) frosting each cookie. Pipe a spiral on each, then draw lines outward from the center with a toothpick, which makes it look like a web.

Web frosting:
- 1 ½ cups powdered sugar
- 2 tbsp. brandy
- ½ tsp. anise extract
- black food coloring

time: 6-8 minutes
temp: 350°
yield: 6 dozen

Loki

Loki was a Norse fire god and a trickster deity. Said to be the blood brother of Odin and the son of a giantess named Laufey. He was both the one at the source of most of the problems of the Aesir gods in Norse myths, and the one to whom the Aesir turned for a solution to those problems. It was Loki who dressed Thor up as Freya and took him to marry the Giant Thrym to reclaim his hammer. Loki was the one who cut off Sif's golden hair, then replaced it with hair of real gold which grew as if it were her hair. He also stole and then recovered Iduna's apples, which kept the gods young, and stole and recovered Freya's necklace. He was the father of Hel, Fenrir and Jormungand.

Lokis

2 tsp. fresh ginger
¾ cup butter
1 egg
2 cups flour
¾ cup brown sugar
½ tsp. baking powder
1 tsp. ground dry ginger
½ tsp. salt
¼ tsp. cloves
(candied ginger or cinnamon candies)

Grate the ginger, cream the wet ingredients including the ginger, mix together the dry ingredients and add them. Form the dough into 2 logs, roll in red and yellow colored sugar. Chill, slice, bake on parchment or lightly greased cookie sheets. You may decorate each cookie with a piece of candied ginger or a cinnamon candy.

time: 12-15 minutes
temp: 350°
yield: 6 dozen

Hel

Hel was the Norse goddess of Helheim, the land of the Dead. She was the eldest of the children of Loki and Angrboda. She is seen as half beautiful woman and half rotting corpse.

Although she is thought of as terrifying, she provided a place and protection for those who died "straw deaths", meaning any death not in battle, such as old age or illness. She was compassionate to those who had been rejected by the rest of society. When Balder and Nana died, she met them with a grand feast and decked her hall with silver and crimson. When Hermod rode down to ask Hel to let them return from her realm, she agreed to let Balder return if everyone in the nine worlds would grieve for him. Unfortunately, some cold-hearted folk refused to weep for him, and so he stayed in Helheim.

Hel's Thumbprints

1 cup ground hazelnuts (filberts)
¼ cup sugar
⅞ cup butter
2 egg yolks
1 tsp. vanilla
2¾ cup flour
¼ tsp. salt
2-4 tbsp. of honey
raspberry jam and powdered sugar

If the hazelnuts are not already roasted, bake them at 350 for 20 minutes. Cool, and then grind them. Mix sugar, butter, egg yolks, vanilla, flour, and salt, then gradually add honey to get the dough to a good moisture for molding. Form into 1" balls, put a thumbprint in each and fill it with a dab of jam. Bake, then dust with powdered sugar.

time: 13-15 minutes
temp: 375°
yield: 40

Odin

At the time of the turn of the last millennium, Odin was the chief of the Aesir, the Norse warrior gods. He was the All-Father, the god of battles, of magic, and of wisdom. While he was a shape-changer, he was often seen as a tall old grey-bearded man with a staff. He was one-eyed, and he had traded one eye for great wisdom, but he wore a wide-brimmed hat which made that point harder to catch.

Odin was credited with creating the world and mankind with his brothers, Vili and Ve. He was a mighty magician, who brought the Runes into the Nine Worlds and taught them to mankind. His spear was called Gungnir, and it never missed its mark. It was a gift from the Dwarves, along with Sif's magical golden hair and Frey's great ship that would hold all the gods, but which he could fold up and put in his pocket.

Odin's Shields

2 cups honey	5 cups flour
1½ cup sugar	1 tbsp. cinnamon
1 tbsp. molasses	½ tbsp. cardamom
2 eggs, beaten	1 tsp. cloves
2 tbsp. lemon juice	½ tsp. nutmeg
2 tsp. lemon peel	1 tsp. salt
1 cup ground almonds	1 tsp. baking soda
Package of fillo dough	

Melt the honey, sugar and molasses together, and let it cool. Sift together the dry ingredients. Mix all the ingredients together, and let cure in a cold place for a week, or at least overnight. It makes a very soft dough. Generously scoop the dough onto cookie sheets lined with fillo dough, and give them plenty of room to spread - no more than six to a sheet. Break off the excess fillo dough after baking (or cut circles to go under each cookie. Decorate each shield with almonds and candied fruit. Glaze with $1/3$ cup sugar dissolved in ¼ cup water.

time: 10-12 minutes
temp: 375°
yield: 30

Sleipnir

Sleipnir was the eight-legged horse of Odin that carried him through the 9 worlds. Sleipnir was the son of Loki and Svadilfari, a fine stallion of the Jotun stonemason, Hrimthurs, who carried the stones to build the walls of Asgard. Loki turned himself into a mare in heat to lure Svadilfari away at the end of the task, so that it would not be completed in time. (Had it been completed on time, the Aesir had promised him the sun, the moon, and Freya.) The ruse worked and the stallion ran off after the mare, not quite finishing the walls. Sadly for Loki, Svadilfari caught up with him, but it was lucky for Odin, who got the swiftest horse in the world from the deal. Odin is often shown riding the Sleipnir with his two ravens Hugin and Munin (Thought and Memory) flying above him.

I suggest carving your own Springerle molds from whatever clean non-resinous wood you can find. You don't need to make Sleipnir, but the traditional springerle design is a horse and rider. Most commercially available modern molds are simple and crude, with little clue what they are supposed to be. I'm sure you can make something no worse.

Sleipnirs

- 4 cups cake flour
- ½ grated lemon peel
- ¼ tsp. anise extract
  OR 4 drops oil of anise
- ½ tsp. bakers ammonia
  OR ¼ tsp. baking powder
- 2 cups sugar
- 4 eggs
- 4 tsp. anise seed (on sheets)

Mix the dough and chill an hour. Roll out dough, dust mold with cornstarch, and press into top of dough. Cut cookies apart and set on cookie sheets sprinkled anise seeds. Let the print dry in overnight - up to 24 hours. Preheat oven to 375, put cookies in and bake. When cool, you can highlight the design with food coloring or petal dust.

time: 15 minutes
temp: 300°
yield: 6 dozen

Runes

The Runes are a magical alphabet, said to have been discovered by Odin through great sacrifice. He hung himself on the great World Tree for nine days, neither eating nor drinking, and at the end of it, discovered the powers of each of the runes. The name of the character set of the Norse runes is called Futhark, as the first letters in it are F U Th A R and K. The later Anglo-Saxon runes are known as Futhorc. Each rune has a special meaning, as well as a sound it represents. With runes, Odin was said to have been able to calm winds, put out fires, dull his enemies' weapons, cause women to fall in love with him, untie fetters, and other magical acts.

After making a full rune set, I like to select the happier runes to mark the balance of the cookies. One *could* use a set of these cookies for divination, if you could grab a cookie without looking at it, but I like to think of it as taking the energy of the rune you select and ingesting it, bringing that energy into yourself, so I lean on Ur, Wynn, Sigil, Dig, Aiwa and other "lucky" runes.

F — wealth
U — strength
Th — thorn
A — message
R — road
K — fire truth
G — gift
W/V — joy
H — hail
N — need
I — ice
Y/J — harvest

Rune Cookies

1 cup honey	3½ cups flour
1 cup brown sugar	1 tsp. cinnamon
2 tbsp. butter	½ tsp. nutmeg
2 tbsp. water	½ tsp. ginger
1 tsp. fresh orange peel	½ tsp. salt
1 cup slivered almonds	½ tsp. soda
4 oz. diced candied orange peel	

Hint: Melt the butter and leave it in the measuring cup, then measure the honey on top. It will help to keep the honey from sticking to the cup.

Melt and mix the wet ingredients together, then the dry ones, reserving 1 cup flour. Mix well. Chill before adding the last cup of flour. This makes a very thick dough. Roll out and cut with a floured knife into 2x2" squares, or cut with a 2-inch round oiled cookie cutter. Cut *before* baking. Press slivered almonds into runes on the tops of the cookies. Bake on greased or lined cookie sheets. Stored in jar or tight tin, they'll last a year. No, really!

time: 9-10 minutes
temp: 400°
yield: 40

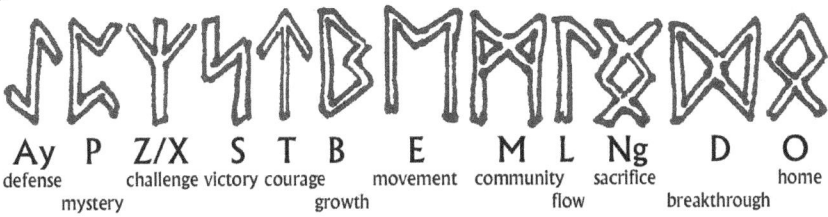

Ay — defense
P — mystery
Z/X — challenge
S — victory
T — courage
B — growth
E — movement
M — community
L — sacrifice
Ng — flow
D — breakthrough
O — home

Frigga

Frigga was the mother goddess of the Aesir, and the goddess of marriage, wives, housewifely arts, childbirth, and peacemaking. Frigga was the wife of Odin, and mother of Balder and Hoder. She could foresee the future, but never told what she saw.

When Frigga foresaw the death of Balder the Beautiful, she went around the world and got promises from every plant and stone that they would never harm him. If anyone threw a weapon at him, it would fly around him instead. This became a game with the gods. However, she neglected to get the mistletoe to make that promise, as it seemed to weak and insignificant. Trouble-making Loki crafted a dart out of mistletoe, and invited Hoder, Balder's blind brother to join the game. The dart struck and killed Balder, despite Frigga's precautions.

Frigga had 12 handmaidens in her hall Fensalir: Eir (healer), Fulla (keeper of treasure), Syn (gate-keeper), Hlin (giver of consolation), Saga (history keeper), Lofn (patron of secret loves), Sjofn (giver of passionate love), Snotra (giver of knowledge), Gna (messenger), Gefion (plough-goddess), Vor (prophetess), Var (enforcer of contracts).

Frigga's Handmaidens

½ cup sugar
9 oz. butter
2 cups flour
1 ¼ cups ground almonds
½ grated lemon rind
2 eggs
1 egg yolk for glazing
(coarse sugar and/or ground almonds)

Mix the dough and chill for an hour. Roll dough 1/8" thick and cut with small cookie cutters, as these are best bite-sized. (If you want to be fancy, you can choose a different shape to represent each of the handmaidens.) Brush lightly with egg yolk glaze and sprinkle with large-crystal sugar before baking, or with a mixture of sugar and ground almonds.

time: 10-12 minutes
temp: 350°
yield: 1/2 gallon

Mimir

Mimir was one of the wisest beings in the Nine Worlds of Norse mythology. He was a mighty giant from Jotunheim, one of the nine worlds (Asgard is the home of the Aesir gods, and Midgard is where the humans live.) Mimir was the guardian of the Well of Wisdom. When Odin sought wisdom he traded his eye for a drink from the well, which was cast into the well. This gave Odin both wisdom and far-seeing.

Mimir, who was the wisest of Odin's councilors, was sent to the Vanir as a hostage after the war between the Aesir and the Vanir, but he refused to teach the Vanir his wisdom, so they cut off his head and sent it back. Odin breathed enough life into it that he was still able to ask Mimir for advice when he needed it.

Mimir's Well Cookies

1 cup sugar
¾ cup butter
1 tsp. baking powder
2 eggs
1 tsp. salt
½ tsp. vanilla

3 cup flour
blueberry preserves

Mix everything but the flour and preserves, then mix in the flour. Form the dough into a ball, and wrap and chill for two hours. Roll out very thin (1/8") and cut into circles about 2½" in diameter. Cut out the centers of half the circles, forming rings. Press the scraps together, and cut and re-roll until there are an equal number of circles and rings. Bake on an ungreased cookie sheet. Let cool, then melt the blueberry preserves (or any other dark preserves), and brush it over the circles, then top with the rings. Sift powdered sugar over the rings.

Time: 10-15 minutes
temp: 350°
yield: 2-3 dozen

Fenris

Fenris (or Fenrir) was a huge wolf, the child of Loki, destined to someday eat the Gods in the time or Ragnarok. To delay this for as long as possible, the Gods decided as Fenris got larger and more dangerous to try to tie him up. But no matter what they tied him with, he would break it as easily as a man breaks a thread. Finally the gods had a magical rope made. It looked thin, but it was made up of such ingredients as the beard of a woman, the roots of a mountain, the sound of a cat's footfall, etc. In order to trick Fenris to let them tie him with this rope, the gods agreed that one of them would put his hand in the Wolf's mouth until he had tried to break it. Since they knew that he would not be able to break it, they knew that whoever put his hand in Fenris's mouth would almost certainly have it bitten off when he discovered that the rope wouldn't break. Only Tyr was brave enough to do that.

These bars were named because of the many and varied ingredients in them which reminded me of the many things it took to make the magic rope that could hold him.

Fenris Bars

½ cup sugar
½ cup butter
1 egg

1 ¼ cup flour
⅛ tsp. salt
½ tsp. vanilla

Mix all these ingredients together and spread and pat them down in 9x12" pan. Bake 15 minutes at 350 degrees while you mix the other ingredients.

When it comes out, spread with:

2 beaten eggs
1½ cup brown sugar
1 cup chopped pecans
½ tsp. baking powder

2 tbsp. flour
1 tsp. vanilla
½ tsp. salt
½ cup coconut

Bake another 25 minutes, and spread with

1 ½ cup confectioners sugar
1 tsp. lemon juice

time: 15 + 25 = 40 minutes
temp: 350°
yield: 20 squares

Tyr

Tyr (or Teiwaz) was the great god of Law and Justice. Tuesday is named for him. In earlier centuries, he was the king of the gods, although later Odin took that place. Tyr is also the name of a T-shaped rune often found carved on ancient sword blades, possibly for victory, possibly for courage or justice. Tyr was the god who put his hand in the mouth of the wolf Fenris, so that he could be bound and the gods could hold off the start of Ragnarok, the End of the World. When Fenris discovered that he could not break the magical rope, he bit off Tyr's hand, as they had all known he would do. Tyr had given his hand up for the good of the world.

Tyr's Hands

½ cup sugar
½ cup molasses
½ cup butter
1½ tsp. soda
¼ tsp. cloves
½ tsp. mace or nutmeg
1 tbsp. grated orange peel

2 cups flour
1 tsp. ginger
½ tsp. cinnamon
1 egg
¼ tsp. salt

Mix all the wet ingredients, and sift together the dry ones (the spices will be much more powerful if you grind them yourself just before baking), and add them to the wet ones. Chill the dough, then roll very thin (1/16"). Cut out with a hand-shaped cookie cutter and bake. When cool you may decorate these with royal icing and cinnamon candies, or eat them plain.

Royal icing: 3 egg whites
  ½ tsp. cream of tartar
Beat stiff, then add:
  1 lb. (4 cups) powdered sugar
This makes rather more royal icing than even I generally use at once, but if well sealed it keeps in the refrigerator for months.

time: 5-7 minutes
temp: 375°
yield: 7 dozen

Freya

Freya, whose name means Lady, was the Norse love goddess of the Vanir, one of the two races of the northern gods. After the war between the Aesir and the Vanir, she was given to the Aesir as a hostage, along with her brother Frey. Freya is the goddess of love, magick, fertility of the fields, and inspiration, and she is also a battle goddess; half of those who are slain in battle come to her hall, Folkvang. Freya drove a chariot drawn by cats, but in battle rode a great golden boar named Hildisvini. As mistress of magick, she flew through the air as a falcon in her feathered cloak. Her greatest treasure is Brisingamen, a gold and amber necklace.

Freya's Cookies

These are recognizable as the popular tarts, Sandbakkels, enjoyed all over Scandinavia. They are served either upside down by themselves, or large ones are filled with fresh berries and topped with whipped cream. If it's not berry season, you can use jam or pie filling. If you can't find good lard, use butter; either is traditional.

> 1½ cup sugar
> 1 cup butter
> 1½ cup lard
> 2 eggs
> 4 cups flour
> ½ tsp. cardamom
> ½ tsp. vanilla
> ¼ tsp. almond extract

Mix the dough. Chill it overnight, press about a tablespoon (or two- depending upon the size) into Sandbakkels tins. Bake in the tins. If you are going to eat them plain without filling them, you can sprinkle them with a mixture of sugar and ground almonds before baking.

time: 8-10 minutes
temp: 350°
yield: 4 dozen

Frey

Frey's name means "Lord". He is the brother of Freya (Lady); they are the children of Njord the sea god. These three gods came from the world of Vanaheim, as hostages after the war between the Aesir (sky/warrior) gods and the Vanir (agricultural) gods. Frey (or Freyr) is a fertility god, patron of sun and rain and bountiful harvests. He's the owner of the ship Skidbladnir, which can hold all the gods, yet be folded up to fit in his pocket. Frey is also the ruler of the elves.

While he is primarily peaceful, he drives a chariot pulled by the golden boar Gullinbursti, and had a magical sword. However, he gave up his sword in order to win his wife Gerda, so when Ragnarok comes, he will face the war without a weapon.

Frey's Cakes

    1 cup sugar
    4 cups flour
    1 tsp. baking powder
    1 cup butter
    1 grated lemon rind
    ¼ lb. bitter almonds
    (OR add 3 tsp. almond extract to
        ¼ lb. normal "sweet" ground almonds)

Mix, chill for an hour, roll into walnut-sized balls, and roll the balls in sugar. Bake on greased or lined cookie sheets.

time: 11 minutes
temp: 350°
yield: 80

Thor

Thor was a great, hearty, red bearded warrior - a great fighter made even more powerful by his great hammer. Thunder was said to be the sound of Thor driving his chariot across the sky. (However he was not allowed to drive across Bifrost, the Rainbow Bridge between Asgard and Midgard, as his power could break or burn it, so he just waded the river that was too deep for everyone else to cross.) His chariot was drawn by two huge goats: Tanngniost (Toothgnasher) and Tanngrisnir (Toothgrinder), which he also was able to kill, and eat when traveling, then bring back to life the next morning to pull the cart again. Once he shared his supper with some fellow travelers, and despite being warned not to, one of the mortals broke a bone to suck the marrow, and the goat was brought back with a limp.

Thor's Goats

2/3 cup sugar
1 cup butter
1 egg yolk
½ tsp. vanilla
1 jigger rum
3 cups flour
1/8 tsp. salt
1 grated lemon rind

Mix, chill, roll 1/4" thick, cut out with goat-shaped cookie cutters, bake on ungreased cookie sheets.

time: 5-7 minutes
temp 400°
yield: 4 dozen

Mjolnir

Mjolnir was Thor's hammer. Loki bet the dwarfs Brokk and Eitri that they couldn't make better treasures than Sif's hair, Odin's spear and Frey's boat. They took the bet, and made Frey's golden boar, and golden ring for Odin, despite Loki taking the form of a horsefly and stinging them as they worked to distract them. But as they were making Thor's hammer, Loki bit Brokk's eye, and although it always struck what it was thrown at and returned to the thrower's hand, the handle was a bit short because Brokk had had to wipe the blood out of his eye.

Mjolnir became the greatest weapon of the gods against the giants, and it was stolen by Thrym, king of the Frost Giants, who offered to trade it back in exchange for marrying Freya. Instead, Loki dressed Thor up like Freya, and managed to keep up the ruse until Thor got his hands on the Hammer again, and killed all the giants at the wedding feast.

Mjolnirs

This is a Speculaas cookie recipe. You can carve a hammer into a piece of wood (or trade a crafty friend cookies for making one for you). Lacking that, you could simply make a cardboard template and cut out hammer-shaped cookies, or use cookie stamps to press designs into the dough before baking.

1 cup sugar
1 cup butter
3 eggs
1 tsp. vanilla
½ tsp. allspice
½ tsp. nutmeg

4½ cups flour
2½ tsp. baking powder
1 tbsp. cinnamon
1 tsp. coriander
½ tsp. cloves
½ tsp. cardamom

1 egg white mixed with ⅓ cup sugar

Mix, chill overnight. Roll the dough ¼ - 3/8" thick. Dust the mold with flour or cornstarch. Press the mold down on the dough, lift off, then cut around the hammer. Bake the hammers. (Try one or two first to check how long to leave them in. The size of the mold will dictate how long they will need to cook.) Brush during the last minute of cooking with an egg white whipped with ⅓ cup sugar.

time: 16 minutes
temp: 350°
yield: 2-6 dozen

The Norns

In Norse mythology, the Norns were the Three Fates, three maidens who lived at the root of the world tree and watered it from the well of Urd, and cared for its roots.

The Norns predicted, and perhaps influenced the Wyrd (destiny) of men and gods. Urd rules what was, Verdandi rules what is now, and Skuld rules what is becoming and could decide life or death for humans. Their duty was to care for the World Tree, to water it, and to smooth clay from the well of Urd (Fate) onto it's roots.

Horn Cakes

½ cup sugar
¾ cup honey
2½ tsp. almond extract
1 lemon rind, grated
½ tbsp. cardamom
½ tbsp. nutmeg
1 tsp. kumquat rind, grated
1 cup blanched chopped almonds
3 cups flour
1 tbsp. cinnamon
2 eggs, beaten
2 oz. ground citron
1 tbsp. baking soda
1½ tsp. rosewater

Melt the sugar into the honey, and let cool. Grate or grind the lemon and kumquat (or orange if you can't find kumquats) rinds and citron. Grind the spices. Mix all the ingredients together, and let the dough cure (sit in a cool place) for several days. Pat the dough onto a cookie sheet ¼" thick, score for cutting later into 2x3" bars, bake. When you take it out, drizzle with lemon glaze:

1 tsp. lemon juice
1½ cup confectioners sugar

Cut into 2x3" bars, and decorate each slice with: candied kumquat or orange rind

time: 15 minutes
temp: 350°
yield: 25

Skadi

Skadi was the goddess of winter, a giantess who loved the mountains, skiing, and all winter sports. Her father was killed by Thor and Loki, and in exchange, she was allowed to choose a husband from the Aesir, but she was only allowed to look at their feet. She chose the feet of who she hoped was handsome Balder, but they turned out to be the feet of Njord, the sea god. Although they tried, their marriage failed. If she lived in Njord's realm, Skadi pined for her mountains, and when they were in Thrymheim, Njord pined for his ocean home. Finally they gave up and separated.

Skadi's Skates

½ cup sugar
1 cup butter
½ tsp. vanilla
2 cup flour
1 cup ground almonds
½ tsp. almond extract

Mix all ingredients and knead together. Chill at least 15 minutes, then roll into ropes, and cut into 4-inch pieces, turning the tips up like skate blades, or skis (not like candy canes).

Brush with:
   1 egg white, whisked softly

Sprinkle with pearl sugar, bake.

time: 15 minutes
temp: 350°
yield: 2 dozen

Mielikki

Mielikki is a Finnish forest goddess. She wears sky-colored stockings and a green coat. Her consort is Tapio who protects plant life and all the green things growing in the forest. Mielikki is the protector of animals, and people living near the forest. She has a bear called Honey Paws, or perhaps that is merely one of her forms. Her child Nyyrikki sends hunters small animals, and her daughter Tyytikki helps people who get lost in the forest.

MIELIKKI BARS

¾ cup sugar
¾ cup cocoa powder
½ cup butter
8 oz. cream cheese
¼ cup sugar
1 egg
¼ cup milk
½ tsp. peppermint extract
green food coloring

With a fork or pastry cutter, cut together sugar, cocoa powder and butter, and press into bottom of 9x9 pan. Bake 15 minutes. Thoroughly blend cream cheese and sugar, then mix in egg, then the other ingredients. Spread over crumb mixture and bake another 10 minutes. Mix a second batch of the chocolate crumbs, but without the food coloring; sprinkle this over the top of the green layer, and bake another 20-25 minutes.

time: (15 + 10 + 20) 45 minutes
temp: 350°
yield: 16

Bastet

Bastet was the most popular goddess of Egypt after Isis. A powerful protector, but also goddess of joy, music, dance and good fortune. Her hieroglyph was of a perfume jar, and she is the goddess of perfume and honey, and the protectress of all cats. She is pictured as a cat, or a woman with a cat's head. In the earliest dynasties, she was a sun goddess, but in later ones she became associated with the moon. Earlier she was described as the daughter of Ra, and he gave her the Uraeus (the Right Eye of Wisdom) for defending him against the serpent Apep during his nightly journey through the underworld. (Horus had the left eye, but there's some confusion there.) Her wrath was legendary.

Bastets

¾ cup butter
⅔ cup oil
⅔ cup sugar
⅔ cup honey
3 eggs
1 tsp. peppermint extract
4 + cups flour
1 tbsp. baking soda
¼ tsp. salt
 assorted paste or powdered food coloring

Mix all the ingredients together and add extra flour tablespoon by tablespoon until the texture of the dough is good for modeling. Divide the dough into portions, kneading a different color into each batch; they should be bright as in Egyptian art. This is a good recipe for kids. Adults may work to make cats, perfume bottles, uraeus, or sistrum; kids will always surprise us. Bake on ungreased sheets until the bottoms just start to brown.

time: 18-20
temp: 300°
yield: 2 dozen (depending upon size)

Ra

Ra (or Re) was the Lord of the Egyptian pantheon. He was a god of the sun, of light and power, the Creator of the world. He was portrayed as a pharaoh with a sun disk on his head. In the beginning Ra rose like the sun and spit forth Shu and Tefnut, who became the first divine couple, and from them all the gods were born. Ra was not as close to humans as his descendants, but preferred to observe from heaven. At night Ra traveled through the underworld in a ship, protected by Set and Mehen. Once Ra and Hathor argued and she left Egypt, and Ra immediately missed her. She changed into a lioness and destroyed anyone who approached her, until Thoth convinced her to return.

Ra Bars

Dough:
- ½ cup sugar
- 1 cup butter
- 2 cups flour
- ½ tsp. baking powder

Mix and bake 25 minutes in 9"x13" pan.

Filling:
- 4 eggs
- $1/3$ cup flour
- 1½ cup sugar
- ½ cup lemon juice
- 1 tsp. lemon peel

Mix well and pour over the cookie layer. Bake another 25 minutes. Cut, dust with powdered sugar. Of course it is much better when made with fresh lemon.

time: 25 + 25 = 50 minutes
temp. 350°
yield: 2 dozen

Isis

Isis was the queen of the Egyptian gods, the faithful wife of Osiris, and the mother of Horus. She had great wings which stretched out over all whom she protected, and on her head was the throne symbol of Osiris, or the horned disk. Isis is the protector of all women and children, and goddess of motherhood, devotion, healing, and magic. She was a water goddess, a sky goddess, an earth goddess and goddess of the underworld. Her worship continued until the 6th century.

Isis was the mightiest of all the Egyptian Pantheon. She restored Osiris to life when he was killed by Set, and restored Horus to life when he had been stung by a scorpion.

Isis Cakes

>¾ cup butter
>½ cup sugar
>½ cup honey
>1 egg
>2 cups flour
>1 tsp. baking powder
>¼ cup sesame seeds

Toast the sesame seeds for 20-25 minutes, until they start to brown. Blend together wet ingredients, then dry, chill, roll, and cut with a 2½" cookie cutter. Smear the top of each cookie with a dab of honey (or apricot jam) and sprinkle sesame seeds over the top. Bake.

time: 13 minutes
temp: 350°
yield: 3 dozen

Osiris

Osiris was the King of the Egyptian gods. He was killed by his brother Set, and his body put into a coffin and thrown into the Nile River. When it landed, a tree grew up around it and was then cut down and used as a roof column in a palace. Isis wandered for years looking for her husband and finally found the column and brought him back to life. But Set killed him yet again, and this time he cut him into 14 pieces and scattered them all over Egypt. Once again Isis went all over collecting the pieces to assemble him again. This time she could not find the last piece, as it had been eaten by a fish. She brought him back to life again, but because one who had died twice could no longer stay in the land of the living, Osiris became the lord of the Underworld.

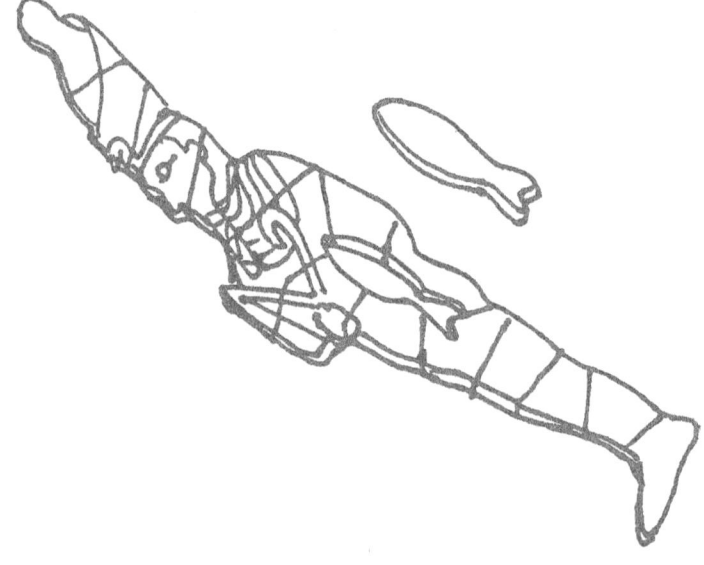

Osiris Puzzle Cookies

1 cup sugar
¾ cup butter
2 eggs
½ tsp. vanilla

3 cups flour
1 tsp. baking powder
1 tsp. salt

Mix all the ingredients together, chill. Roll 1/4" thick. Make a cardboard template and lay it on the dough and cut around it (and develop a great appreciation for cookie cutters). Use a fish-shaped cookie cutter to cut out a piece in the middle of the cookie, then use a knife to cut inward to divide the cookie into 14 pieces. Paint decoration on after cutting, but before baking with egg paint with paint brushes (kept in a special place just for cooking).

For egg paint, mix:
    1 egg yolk
    1 tbsp. water

Divide evenly into four saucers or small cups and stir red, yellow, green, blue liquid food coloring to each to make your palette. Bake after painting. Extra dough can be rolled and cut into cartouches. Make sure they don't over bake - they should be just barely browned on the bottom so the colors will stay clear.

time: 5-7 minutes
temp: 400°
yield: 4 dozen

Hathor

Hathor was an Egyptian Mother goddess. She is shown as a woman with a cow's head or horns. When Ra became old the people of Egypt became disrespectful and mocked him, disobeying his laws. So he called The Eye of the Sun, and she became Sekhmet the lioness, who went out and slew the people of Egypt. Ra looked down on the slain people and felt pity, but not even he could stop Sekhmet. But he could trick her. He had 7,000 jars of beer brewed and colored with red ochre and poured this 9 inches deep over the place where Sekhmet was coming to kill in the morning. When she got there, she saw the land covered with what she thought was the blood of those she had slain. Laughing, she began to drink the beer. When 24 hours had passed without her killing one person, Ra was able change her name to Hathor, and changed her nature to sweetness. Henceforth she would lay men and women low with the power of love. Her symbols are incense, jewels, mirrors, cosmetics, sistra (a sistrum is a musical instrument shaped like an Ankh with bells in it) and other musical instruments, milk, honey and of course, beer.

Hathor's Sistra

> ½ cup sugar
> 1 ¼ cup flour
> ⅓ cup cocoa
> ½ cup butter
> 1 egg white
> ½ tsp. peppermint extract

Mix, chill, make into 2 dozen sistra. These look like Ankhs. Bake on greased or lined cookie sheets, and cool.

Make icing:
> 2 cups powdered sugar
> 2 egg whites
> ¼ tsp. cream of tartar
> ½ tsp. peppermint mint extract
> green food coloring

Mix, thin with water to consistency of cake batter. Dip the sistra in the frosting to coat; dry on racks.

time: 5-10 minutes
temp: 325°
yield: 2 dozen

Bes

Bes was the Egyptian god of good luck, marriage blessings, and laughter. He also protected children, especially by killing snakes. He was seen as an ugly little dwarf, but he made folk laugh, so he was a beloved god. He also helped women in childbirth, and was a fertility god.

Bes Cookies

½ cup powdered sugar
¾ cup butter
1 tbsp lemon rind
1 cup flour
½ cup cornstarch

Mix all 5 ingredients together, and form into a log about a foot long. Roll the log in colored sugar spread on a sheet of waxed paper. When the sugar is thickly pressed in, wrap the roll in waxed paper and store it (for up to three months) in the freezer. Or you can just chill it, then either thaw (if frozen) or slice thin, bake, cool. Before baking, when the slices are on the cookie sheet, you can snip out a star-shaped stencil and, placing it over each cookie, make a color sugar star on each. You can cut any simple symbol carefully from heavy plastic film with a stencil-cutting knife, and save the stencil right in your cookbook. (Wipe it before putting it away).

time: 10-12 minutes
temp. 375°
yield: 3½ dozen

HERMES

Hermes was a son of Zeus, and Maia, and the messenger of the gods. The Romans knew him as Mercury, and he wore winged sandals and a winged hat. Known for both the speed of his travel and the speed of his wit, he protected travelers, merchants, shepherds, and thieves. The very morning he was born he slipped out of the cave where his mother was sleeping and stole some of Apollo's cows; that afternoon he killed a turtle, and using its shell and intestines from the cows, created the first lyre. He used the lyre to placate Apollo (the god of music) for stealing his cows.

HERMES' COINS

½ cup sugar
½ cup honey
1 cup butter
1 egg
1 tsp. vanilla
2 cups flour
¼ tsp. baking powder
½ tsp. salt

Mix wet ingredients, then add in dry. Roll, cut out. Cut small rounds to look like coins, cool, frost, and dip into orange or yellow sugars, or paint with gold, silver and copper petal dust. (Or use whatever cutters you like.)

Icing:
    1 cup powdered sugar
    2 tbsp. butter
    ¼ tsp. grated orange peel
    yellow/orange decorating sugars
      OR petal dust

time: 12 minutes
temp: 350°
yield: 5 dozen

JANUS

Janus was the Roman god of coming and going, of the past and the future, of the spaces "between"; the modern word "janitor" comes from his name. Janus was also the God of doorways. Images of his head were often put on doorways as a guardian. He was pictured with two faces, one looking back gaining wisdom from the past, and one looking forward into the future.

He was invoked at the start of any enterprise, along with whichever god or goddess would patronize the specific activity.

JANUS COOKIES

    2 egg whites
    ½ tsp. vanilla
    ½ tbsp orange extract
    ½ tsp. finely grated orange peel
    ¼ tsp. cream of tartar
    ½ cup superfine sugar

This is a meringue cookie (very good for using up extra egg whites), light and sweet. Whip the egg white with the cream of tartar until stiff, then beat in the sugar and orange flavoring.

Pipe two curls, representing the two faces of the god, onto baking parchment or brown paper bags. They bake very slowly - meringues are more dehydrated than baked, and I usually put them in at the end of a baking cycle. They can be made ahead and frozen, but are very susceptible to humidity, and are fragile.

time: 2 hours
temp: 200°
yield: 2-3 dozen

PAN

Pan was known as the Goat-Footed God, with horns and the hind quarters of a goat (although more urbane gods would also say he had the manners and appetites of a goat as well). He was a god of wild places, and wild feelings. The word "panic" comes from the terror that comes upon men when they are alone in wild places and hear Pan playing. He is a great musician, especially on the pipes, and fond of dancing, drinking and partying. Pan is friend of all animals, wild and domestic, and those who care for them, and lord of fauns and satyrs. Panpipes were a series of pipes of different lengths bound together.

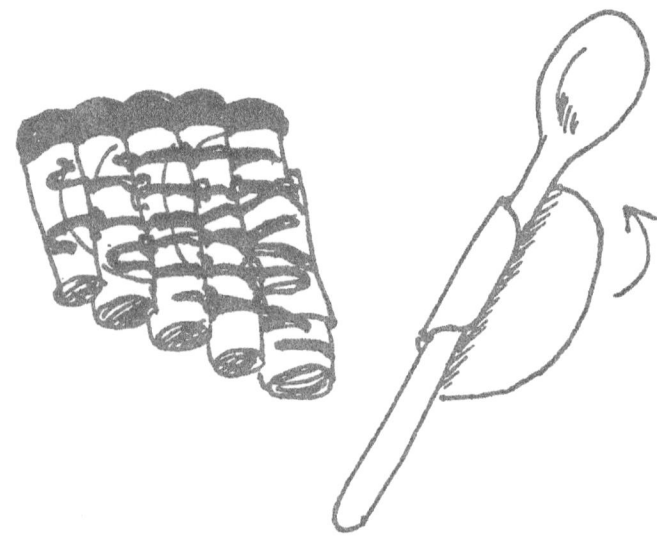

PAN PIPES

½ cup sugar
3 egg whites
1½ tsp. vanilla
2 tsp. butter
6 oz. semi-sweet chocolate

½ cup + 1 tbsp flour
1 tbsp orange peel
¼ cup butter, melted

Prepare greased cookie sheets; if you have to re-use any, make sure they are cooled between batches. Beat the sugar and egg whites until stiff, gradually fold in the flour and other ingredients, the butter last. Drop spoons full of batter onto cookie sheets 4" apart, and spread thinly. Try to have them as evenly flat as possible. Vary them between 2 and 4 inches in diameter. Bake the cookies one sheet at a time, and when they come out, roll each around the handle of a wooden spoon. This goes pretty quickly if you have a team working. When you have a series of tubes, melt 6 oz semi-sweet chocolate and 2 tsps. butter together. Then dip or paint the dark chocolate on the sides of the tubes to stick them together in a graduated line with one end even. If there is leftover chocolate when they are all assembled, drizzle it decoratively over the top to look like the bindings holding the pipes together.

time: 3-4 minutes per sheet
temp: 425°
yield: ~ 1 dozen

APHRODITE

Aphrodite, the Greek Goddess of Love and Beauty, was born of sea foam when drops of blood from the death of Uranus fell into the waves. She is married to Hephaestus, the lame smith god. She has many lovers including Zeus, Ares, and the mortal man Adonis. Her son with Ares is Eros, the god of Love with his bow and arrows. Apples, roses, poppies, doves, swans, rams and April are sacred to her. The Romans knew her as Venus.

APHRODITE'S DOVES

2 egg whites
½ tsp. vanilla
½ cup superfine sugar
¼ tsp. cream of tartar

Make meringue, beat egg whites and cream of tartar until it forms stiff peaks, then gradually beat in the sugar and fold in the vanilla. Put the meringue in a pastry bag and pipe a tight S with a back-loop to form the wing. You can practice on waxed paper until you have the hang of it, then put it back into the bag, and pipe onto parchment or brown paper bags. Swans can be made by elongating the neck. Add eyes and beak with miniature chocolate chips. Bake.

time: 1 hour
temp: 200°
yield: 5-6 dozen

DEMETER

Demeter was the goddess of fertility and agriculture. When Hades abducted her daughter Persephone, she wandered in misery and nothing would grow as she was not nourishing it. Mankind was dying, so Zeus forced Hades to allow Persephone return to earth, providing she had eaten nothing while in the land of death. However, Persephone had already eaten six pomegranate seeds, so she had to return to Hades for half the year to be Queen of the Dead. During that time, plants wither, and that's why we have winter. When Persephone returns to her the surface, spring and summer return.

Demeter's symbols are the poppy and the crane. Persephone's are mint, asphodel, and, of course, pomegranate.

Kore (Maiden) is the title given to Persephone in the Eleusinian Mysteries. There are many statues in museums of ladies with mysterious smiles known only as Kores.

KORES

½ cup butter
¾ cup sugar
1 egg
1 egg yolk
1 tsp. vanilla
½ tsp. lemon extract
2 cups flour
1 tsp. baking powder
2 tbsp. poppy seeds

Mix all the ingredients together, place in a covered bowl and chill until firm. Form dough into 2½" crescents on lined pan. (Using baking parchment is good.) Bake, cool, and sprinkle with powdered sugar.

time: 12 minutes
temp: 350°
yield: 2 dozen

ARTEMIS

Artemis is the Greek goddess of the hunt and the protector of wild things. She is the daughter of Zeus and Leto. Immediately after she was born, she got up and played midwife to her twin brother Apollo, so she is a goddess of childbirth even though she is a virgin. She asked her father for permission to remain unmarried all her life, and spends her time hunting and protecting animals - especially bears, bees, goats, lions, and bulls.

She was very independent, and not gentle. When the young hunter Actaeon saw her bathing in the river, she turned him into a stag and his own hounds hunted him down and killed him. Another time she became fond of the hunter Orion, but her brother Apollo was jealous and challenged her to hit a tiny target with her bow and arrows, far out to sea. She did, but it sadly turned out to be the head of Orion, so she placed him into the sky where he remains today as the constellation of Orion.

BOWS OF ARTEMIS

    1 cup sugar
    1 cup butter
    1-2 egg yolks
    ¼ cup sour cream
    2½ cups flour
    1 tsp. baking powder
    1 tsp. cinnamon
    1 tsp. lemon rind

Mix the dough, chill, roll into thin rods and form into bow shapes. If you cross each with an arrow on it, they will be sturdier, or you can pipe them with a cookie gun. (Do not expect them to stay thin, they spread, but the point is the taste!) Brush with egg wash, sprinkle with finely chopped almonds and pearl sugar or crushed sugar cubes.

time: 10-15 minutes
temp: 375°
yield: 2 dozen

HECATE

Hecate was a pre-Olympian goddess, although she came to complete the Greek agricultural-goddess trinity with Persephone and Demeter. Hecate symbolized the harvested corn which is no longer "alive", containing the potential for rebirth. She is often shown as the one incorporating all three forms of the Divine Feminine. She was the handmaiden of Artemis and a goddess of the Underworld.

She is a lunar goddess, a protectress, destroyer, and magician. Crossroads, especially places where three roads meet, are sacred to her. As with other Great Goddesses, she has many symbols. Her animals are usually dogs, wolves, lions, bears, snakes, owls, and spooky animals associated with the night. She is sometimes shown with three heads, a dog, a snake and a horse, or with a three-headed dog. Her other symbols include torches, keys, rope, and knives. Her plants are those which are dangerous, that can kill or cure: aconite, yew, hemlock, and willow. Midwives are under her special protection.

HECATE'S MOONS
(or hounds or torches depending on the shape)

1½ cups sugar	5 cups flour
1 cup butter	½ tbsp. baking soda
¾ cup boiling water	½ tbsp. cardamom
1 tsp. ginger	1 tsp. cinnamon
½ tsp. cloves	

Sift together the dry ingredients, cream together the sugar and butter, mix in the flour, then add the boiling water, and mix well. This makes a soft dough, so refrigerate, then roll and cut out (Hecate has so many symbols, you should be able to find a cutter for some of them). Or cut 1½" circles, then cut half of them in half, and gently press two half moons on the sides of each "full moon". Bake on greased or lined cookie sheets. Decorate shaped cookies with icing and cinnamon candies. These cookies are very thin and crunchy, and make good ornaments if you pierce them with a straw before baking and hang with a ribbon.

For royal icing, blend:
  2 egg whites
  ¼ tsp. cream of tartar
  2 cups powdered sugar.

time: 5-7 minutes
temp: 375°
yield: 5 dozen

ATHENA

Athena is the virgin Greek goddess of war, peace, literature and all useful arts, especially weaving. She is the daughter of Zeus and Metis, the goddess of intelligence. Fearing a child that would supplant him as he had supplanted his father, Zeus tricked Metis into turning into a fly and swallowed her. Inside his head, she forged armor for Athena, and this gave Zeus such a headache that he had Hephaestus break his head open with a hammer. Athena sprang out fully grown and armed. She gave mankind the olive tree, and taught them agriculture, weaving and many crafts. While she is a warrior goddess, she is the goddess of tactics, not carnage. The olive tree and the owl – the bird of wisdom - is her symbol.

Although she is the goddess of wisdom and refuses to marry, she is a bit vain. She participated in the competition for the Golden Apple, which led to the fall of Troy. Another time, after inventing the flute, when she saw herself playing it, she didn't like how her cheeks puffed out and threw it away, where it was picked up by Pan. When she realized that the weaver Arachne was a better weaver than she was, Athena turned her into a spider.

ATHENA'S OWLS

1½ cup sugar
1 cup butter
1 egg
8 oz. cream cheese
1 tsp. vanilla
½ tsp. almond extract
3½ cups flour
1 tsp. baking powder

Mix ingredients, chill, roll out 1/8" thick. Cut with owl-shaped cookie cutters, or into circles and stamp in owls so they will look like the coins of ancient Athens (and modern Euros). If you can't find one, you can make a stamp with oven baked "clay". Bake on ungreased or lined cookie sheets.

time: 8-10 minutes
temp: 375°
yield: ~ 90

AMALTHEA

Amalthea was the name of the goat who nursed Zeus when his mother hid him from his father, Chronos the Titan. Chronos, worried that his son would dethrone him as he had dethroned his father, asked his wife Rhea to give him their children when they were born, and then he swallowed them all. Rhea, tired of this after five children, gave her husband a rock to swallow when Zeus was born, and hid him in a cave on Crete. There he was cared for by the magical goat Amalthea who gave him milk, and hung his cradle in a tree so he would be found neither in heaven nor on earth. One of her horns came off and the broken horn became the Horn of Plenty, always pouring forth a limitless supply of food.

AMALTHEA'S HORNS

½ cup butter
1 egg yolk
¾ cup sour cream
2 cups flour
1 teaspoon cinnamon
¼ cup sugar

These are more like pastry than cookies. Cut the butter into small bits and stir into the flour. Process until there are no more visible lumps, then add the sour cream and egg yolk. Be careful not to overwork the dough. Form the dough into two balls, wrap and chill, roll them out into 12-inch circles and spread with cinnamon sugar. Cut each circle into 12 wedges, then roll up and curl into crescents. Bake on lined pans.

time: 25 minutes
temp: 350°
yield: 24

POTNIA

Potnia (which means Mistress) was a Cretan mother goddess. Her symbol was the Double Axe, or Labrys. The Labrys is said to represent the waxing and waning moon. The Mycenaean culture on Crete was matriarchal; there seems to have been no male god, not even a consort or son. Figures of Potnia and the double axe were found until later periods, after the patriarchal Greeks had conquered Crete. Potnia's cult objects also included snakes, birds, horns, bulls, but none are referred to in writings when writing was developed.

LABRYS COOKIES

¼ cup superfine sugar
½ cup butter
¼ tsp. ground coriander
¼ tsp. ground fennel
1 cup white flour
½ cup rice flour

This is a basic shortbread, with the spices sacred to Potnia added. Rub the butter into the flours, then beat in the sugar and spices. Roll out and cut in circles, then cut the circles in two, and place them back to back to form the labrys shape.

time: 40-45 minutes
temp: 325°
yield: 12

GAEA

Gaea/Gaia is the Greek Great Earth Mother, wife and Mother of Uranus, and mother of the all the Titans, Cyclops and Hecatoncheires (hundred handed ones).

The name Gaea is now used to describe the whole Earth as a living entity, as discussed in the Gaea Hypothesis. There are many scientists who have come to the conclusion that there seems to be some overall consciousness which springs from the Earth herself.

GAEAS

2 cups flour
1 cup powdered sugar
1 cup butter
1 tsp. fresh orange peel
1 cup chopped pistachios
4 ounces dark chocolate
¼ cup chopped pistachios
(optional- green food coloring)

Mix the flour sugar and butter, add the orange peel and the chopped pistachios. Form into 1" balls, bake. Melt the chocolate in a Pyrex measuring cup in the microwave. Spread the top of the balls with the melted dark chocolate and sprinkle with chopped pistachios.

time: 8-10minutes
temp: 375°
yield: 6 dozen

BEAN TIGHE

Bean Tighe (pronounced Bantee) means woman of the house. She is pictured as an older woman, who keeps an eye on the house, may help with chores, take care of the animals, and especially watch children. She is rarely seen, but occasionally heard sweeping. The Bean Tighe is very fond of strawberries and cream. If you want to see if you have one, leave a piece of linen drying by the fire, and if it is turned when no one is looking, you may have attracted a Bean Tighe.

BEAN TIGHE STARS

>   1 cup sugar
>   1 cup butter
>   1 egg
>   1 tsp. vanilla
>   2½ cup flour
>   ½ tsp. salt
>   (Strawberry jelly or preserves)

Mix, chill, roll out thinly, cut with star cookie cutter. Cut a round hole in the center of half of these. Place non-pierced cookies on greased cookie sheets. Warm strawberry jelly, and spread over the center of each star, top with pierced tops, with star points non-aligned. If you have home made strawberry preserves, it's nice to have a large piece of strawberry in the center of each. Bake.

time: 8-10 minutes
temp. 350°
yield: 3 dozen

BRIGIT

Brigit was the great Goddess of the Celtic people. Fire of the forge, fire of inspiration, and fire of the hearth were all sacred to her, as were many springs and wells. The Brigit's cross - a sign of the sun - was made of rushes or straw, and hung around the house on Bride's day (February 2), when the last year's crosses were burned. The Goddess Brigit was the child of the Dagda, and the Goddess of healers, fires, smiths and everything to do with fire, the arts, poetry, fertility, midwives, livestock (especially cows), and the creator of the Ogham alphabet.

Brighit was so popular that she was transformed into Saint Brigit, the child of a king and a slave, born neither inside nor outside (on the doorstep), as she was not to be fitted into any category. She was said to have been the midwife to the Virgin Mary, and created a community of women in Kildare who kept an eternal flame burning, most likely a continuation of a pagan shrine. The abbey still exists today.

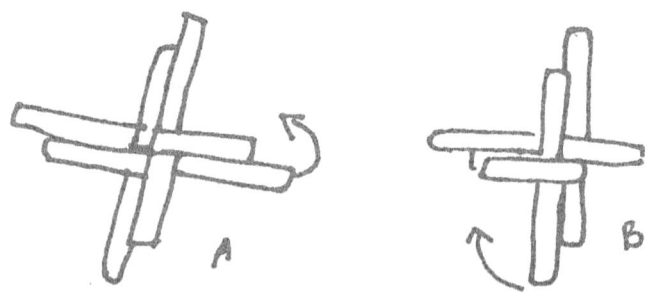

BRIGIT'S CROSSES

1 tbsp. sugar
2 tbsp. butter
2 eggs
¼ cup milk

2 cups flour
½ tsp. salt
½ tsp. baking powder

Mix dough, knead, let stand 20 minutes. Form into 16 balls, stretch and roll to flatten each to a "paper thin" rectangle, and cut each into 4 strips, fairly well floured. Fold each in half, and insert the folded edge between the legs of another, then insert another into that one, until you have locked all four together in a Bridgits cross. (Experiment with strips of paper first!) Trim the ends to make the arms 3½". When they are all formed, fry them in corn oil about one to two inches deep, heated until a piece of bread or scrap of dough tossed in cooks quickly. Fry about 2-3 at a time. Glaze with 1 tsp. lemon in ½ cup honey.

oil temp: 365°
yield: 16

THE DAGDA

The Dagda means simply The Good God. The Dagda was the high king of the Tuatha De Danann. He was the God of death and rebirth, and trades. He had the great cauldron that gave limitless food, and a harp that kept the seasons in the right order when he played it. He was pictured with a great club which he could kill nine men with one blow, or restore them to life by touching them with the other end of it.

BAGDA'S CLUBS

    ¼ cup brown sugar
    1 cup butter
    1 tsp. vanilla
    1 tbsp. water
    1½ cup + 2 tbsp. flour
    6 tbsp. ground almonds
    5 tbsp. ground hazelnuts
    5 tbsp. ground pecans

Mix gently, form into long balls, slightly tapered to look like clubs. Bake on ungreased cookie sheets then roll in superfine sugar while still warm.

time: 15 minutes
temp: 350°
yield: 4 dozen

THE MORRIGAN

The Morrigan was the Celtic death goddess- goddess of war, prophecy, and passion. With Badb and Macha, the Morrigan formed another triad of goddesses. She was called the Battle Raven, and the Washer at the Ford. The Dagda is said to meet with Morrigan at the ford at Samhain (Halloween), combining the forces of destruction with fertility. Her sacred animals are the cow, mare, raven and crow; her colors are red and black. She is the essence of the scary power of women, and while men come to her for victory, it may be wonderful, but never safe.

This is my favorite brownie recipe, overdone by adding more. Cut in smaller pieces than you would with normal brownies.

Death by Chocolate Brownies

2 cups sugar
1 cup flour
¾ cup butter
¾ cup cocoa powder
4 eggs
pinch salt
1 tsp. vanilla
2 cups semi-sweet chocolate chips
½ cup chopped nuts (optional)
¼ cup each white and milk chocolate chips
½ tsp. Godiva liqueur (optional)

Mix in order: sugar and butter, eggs, vanilla, flour, cocoa powder (preferably Sparrow brand), salt, nuts (I like pecans best), and 1 cup of the semi-sweet chocolate chips. Bake in a buttered pan for about 1/2 hour. When they come out, dump 1 cup of semi-sweet chocolate chips over the top- when they soften, smooth the melted chocolate over the top of the brownies. Scatter the white and milk chocolate chips over the melted dark chocolate, and let cool. If they soften too, you can swirl them for a marbled look to the chocolate "icing".

time: ~30 minutes
temp: 350°
yield: 9x13 pan, approx 24 deadly brownies

RHIANNON

Rhiannon, part of the Celtic triple goddess, was also written of in the Mabinogion and Arthurian romances, where she became the wife of King Pwyll of Dyfed. Pwyll (pronounced Poo-ul) sees Rhiannon riding a white horse, and first sends others, then tries to catch up with her himself. However, although it appears that she is riding slowly, no one can catch up to her even when they ride their horses as fast as they can. Finally when the king's horse is exhausted, Pwyll calls out and asks for her to wait for him, and she stops immediately, pointing out that it would have been easier on his horse, if he'd tried asking before then.

Various symbols of Rhiannon include the moon, horseshoes, daffodils, pansies, hummingbirds, songbirds, badgers.

WAFERS OF RHIANNON

    ¾ cup brown sugar
    ½ cup margarine
    1 egg
    ½ tsp. vanilla
    1 ¾ cup flour
    ¾ tsp. cardamom
    ½ tsp. cinnamon
    ¼ tsp. salt

Mix, chill the dough, form into 1" balls, stamp balls with a cookie stamp in a design with one of her many symbols, making them as thin as you can. Bake on a greased cookie sheet.

time: 8 minutes
temp: 350°
yield: 96

THE CELTIC TRIPLE GODDESSES

The Celtic version of the triple Goddess is Blodeuwedd as Maiden, Arianrhod as Mother, and Cerridwen as Crone. Blodeuwedd was created out of flowers by the wizard Math to be a bride for Llew of the Silver Hand.

Arianrhod is the goddess of the Silver Wheel, the moon. She is a goddess of the seasons, time and tides, and weaves the destinies of men. She was the daughter of the great Mother Don, sister of the magician Gwydion; she was the virgin mother of the twins Llew and Dylan (light and darkness). She dwells in Caer Sidi, where she cares for souls between incarnations, and shooting stars are said to be souls returning to earth from Caer Sidi to be reborn.

Cerridwen is the Great Mother of the bard Taliesin. She is a goddess of birth, death, inspiration and arts, science and magic. Her symbols are the white sow and the cauldron of inspiration.

SILVER WHEELS

¾ cup sugar
¾ cup butter
1 egg
1 tsp. vanilla
1 cup ground almonds
2 cups flour
½ tsp. baking powder
½ tsp. salt
1 tsp. lemon peel

Mix, roll ¼" thick, cut moons, and bake. Sift powdered sugar over cooled cookies. If you wish to celebrate Cerridwen, you can cut the cookies with cauldron-shaped or pig shaped cookie cutters, or use flower-shaped cutters for Blodeuwedd.

time: 8-9 minutes
temp: 350°
yield: 5 dozen

BLODEUWEDD

Blodeuwedd was a beautiful woman created out of flowers by the great magician Math to be the wife of Llew, but she became tired of him and tried to kill him, so she was punished by being turned into an owl. Her symbols are the moon and the owl, and also the flowers the made her: bean, burdock, meadowseet, primrose, nettle, hawthorn, oak and chestnut.

BLODEUWEDD'S FLOWERS

    1 cup butter
    2 cups flour
    $1/3$ cup heavy cream
    1 cup sugar for rolling

Cut the butter into the flour, and moisten with the cream. Gather the dough into a ball and chill. Roll dough 1/8" thick and cut with tiny flower shaped cutters (1 ¼"). Spread sugar on waxed paper and turn flowers in it on both sides, prick each cookie with a fork 2-3 times, and bake. Beat together cream filling. Divide cream into three or four batches and tint each with food coloring - pink, blue, yellow, green, violet - whatever you like. When wafers are cool, sandwich with creme.

Filling:
    ¾ cup butter
    ¾ cup powdered sugar
    1 egg yolk
    1 tsp. vanilla
    food coloring

time: 7-9 minutes
temp: 375°
yield: ~ a hundred

EPONA

Epona was a Gallo-Celtic Horse Goddess. She was usually shown riding a horse or with a fruit basket or cornucopia. Pigs were sacrificed to her, and her shrines decorated with rose garlands. The Roman added her to their pantheon when they spread into Gaul and Britain; there was said to be an Epona shrine in "every stable" in the Empire. In England Epona was associated with Macha and Rhiannon.

EPONA'S HORSES

1½ cups sugar
2 cups butter
2 eggs
1 tsp. vanilla
5 cups flour
2 tsp. baking powder
¼ tsp. salt
2 tbsps. milk

Mix the flour, sugar, butter, baking powder, salt, eggs and vanilla. Take ¼ of the dough, add milk, and beat until thin enough to pipe. Separate it into at least 3 or 4 parts and add food coloring to each.

Chill the rest of the dough until firm, roll 1/4 " thick, cut with horse-shaped and cornucopia cookie cutters. Decorate enthusiastically with piped colors. This makes a colorful sugar cookie without all that gooey frosting. Bake on a ungreased cookie sheet.

time: 6-8 minute
temp: 375°
yield: 4 dozen

HERNE

Herne the Hunter is a name for the ancient Horned God. As the Green Man rules and represents the vegetation, the Horned God is the lord of animals. They existed before named gods- they are more "powers" than entities. Herne is sometimes seen as a powerful stag, and other times as a horned man. He is both the hunted and the hunter, the Lord of the Forest. He reminds us that we are part of the animal kingdom.

There's also an English legend about Herne the Hunter, a hunter of Richard the Second who saved his master's life from a stag at bay, but was wounded in the process. A stranger appeared who tied the antlers to his head, miraculously saving his life. However, the cost was his hunting skill, so he hanged himself from an oak. Afterwards, his ghost was said to lead the Wild Hunt across the King's forests to chase down and punish the unjust.

HERNE'S BEASTS

½ cup molasses
²/₃ cup brown sugar
3 tbsp. lard
1½ tsp. orange extract
¾ tsp. soda mixed into 1 tsp. hot water
2-3 cups flour
½ tsp. ground cinnamon
½ tsp. ground ginger
½ tsp. ground cloves
½ tsp. ground mace

This is a Moravian recipe. Melt together the molasses, brown sugar, and lard. Let cool, then mix in the orange extract, and the baking soda in water. Sift together the dry ingredients and mix in. Knead well. Let the dough "ripen" (sit covered in a cool place) for several days. Roll "tissue paper thin", cut in animal shapes, bake on greased or lined cookie sheets. Watch carefully so that they don't over-brown.

time: 7 minutes
temp: 350 °
yield: ~ a whole lot

Beltane

Beltane is the pre-Christian celebration of May Day, the first of May. It's halfway between the Vernal Equinox and the Summer Solstice. Traditionally it is celebrated with balefires or bonfires on May Eve, and going into the woods to pick flowers and branches to decorate the houses, and dancing around Maypoles. Ashes from the Belfires (or Balefires) are smudged on the forehead and sprinkled on the fields. All other fires are put out, and re-lighted from the community fire. Rowan branches were placed in windows, and the youngest member of the family would pick a primrose and place it on the doorstep for protection. Folk danced around and leapt over the fires for fertility, and one girl was chosen Queen of the May (a living representative of the goddess of love).

Beltane Flowers

1 1/3 cup sugar	3 cups flour
2/3 cup butter	1 tsp. cream of tartar
2 eggs	1 tsp. baking soda
1/2 tsp. vanilla	1/2 tsp. salt
4 tbsp. milk	1/4 tsp. lemon extract

Mix. chill, roll, cut into assorted-size flowers (or stars, which are easier to find). Bake on ungreased sheets. Cool. Decorate by icing white and then painting on concentric stars with liquid food coloring, and then add a dragee in the center of each one.

icing: 1 cup sifted powdered sugar
　　　1/4 tsp. clear "vanilla" extract
　　　assorted food colors
　　　lemon juice

Sift the powdered sugar, and add the vanilla (this is the only time I will put up with artificial vanilla, because real vanilla produces a beige icing). Add one teaspoon of lemon juice at a time until the icing is a good spreading consistency. When all cookies are coated, you can divide the rest and tint it to paint with, or paint with coloring simply diluted with water.

time: 7 - 9 minutes
temp: 375°
yield: about 100

#

The Green Man is the Great Spirit of the forest, specifically the plants, as the Horned God is of animals. The Green Man is associated with summer; he was often one of the traditional characters, like Punch and the hobby horse who danced with the Morris Dancers. Also called Jack i' the Green, he is a fertility character; Jack dances inside a conical framework covered with leaves, and is a version of the Fool from the Tarot.

He has also been associated with the Green Knight in the Arthurian legend who offered to exchange blows with any of Arthur's knights. Sir Gawain offered, and chopped off his head, but the Green Knight picked it up and walked away. A year later, Sir Gawain went to his castle and allowed the knight to strike his neck, surviving with magical help from the knight's lady.

GREEN MAN NUT BALLS

²/₃ cup sugar
1 ¾ cup flour
1 cup butter
1 egg
¼ tsp. baking powder
1 tsp. almond extract
½ tsp. salt
½ cup chopped pistachios

Chop the pistachios, mix all other ingredients into a dough, and chill for an hour. Roll into 1" balls, bake, cool, decorate the cookies with icing and more chopped nuts. They don't really need the icing, but it makes them even better.

Icing:
    1 cup powdered sugar
    2 tbsp. milk
    ¼ tsp. grated lemon peel

Sprinkle the wet icing with the chopped pistachios.

time: 15-18 minutes
temp: 350°
yield: 4½ dozen

The Green Man II

The Green Man is a lord of vegetation, the spirit of all plant life. He is shown as a wild man of the forest clothed in leaves, and sometimes even with leaves growing out of his hair or mouth. Green Men are found carved in church decoration all over England and other places in Europe - not usually prominently, but tucked in corners, or on misericord seats with other grotesques. He may be a version of John Barleycorn, the spirit of the grain who is cut down and comes back again when the grain grows each year, and makes men merry when he turns into "nut brown ale".

No Bake Green Men

A "no-bake" recipe seemingly designed to burn children's fingers.

½ cup butter
4 cup cornflakes
3 cups marshmallows
1 tsp. vanilla
1½ tsp. green food color
nonpareils/dried fruit/various small candies

Melt butter in saucepan, then stir in and melt marshmallows, add food coloring and vanilla, then cornflakes (you could also use wheat flakes). Cool until just safe to handle, then drop spoonfuls on wax paper. Form (or let the kids form) Green Man faces on waxed paper. Use red candies or bits of candied cherries for the mouths and nonpareils (the large silver kind) or candied fruit for the eyes. Let harden.

Try to keep the cookies small enough so that the mouths seem at least a little in scale with the faces. If they get too big the cornflakes look more like moss and less like leaves and the eyes disappear. While forming, keep the mixture gooey by sitting the pan in a larger pan of warm water. You could also use Nerd candies for the eyes, or I suppose, the new tiny blue M&Ms. This would allow you to make a larger cookie.

yield: maybe 3 dozen, depending on the kids.

Litha

Also known as "midsummer", this is the celebration of the Summer Solstice, the longest day of the year. It is celebrated with bonfires on hill tops and maypoles and used to be celebrated by rolling barrels, wheels and other large round objects *set on fire* down hills into bodies of water. Another tradition is to stay up all night on this shortest night of the year, sometimes dancing all night.

These are, of course, the small cakes usually known as Madelines. These simple cakes baked in shell-shaped molds combine the virtue of only needing 12 minutes to cook with the aquatic theme of the Summer Solstice. If you do not have Madeline pans, you can use cupcake tins, but then they look more like full moons than sea shells.

Litha Shells

    ½ cup stick of butter (not margarine!)
    ½ cup white sugar
    ½ cup white flour
    1 egg
    1 tsp. rum extract

Preheat oven and butter madeline pans generously with stick of butter. This will use up about a quarter of the stick. In small pan over medium heat, melt the rest of the butter, stirring well. As soon as it is melted, take the pan from the heat, and add the sugar directly into it; stir in. This should cool it enough to stir in the egg without cooking it. Then add the rum (or whatever extract you prefer) and the flour. Mix quickly and spoon into the pans, bake. (You can double this if you have two pans, but make separate batches if you want to more than double it.)

time: 12 minutes
temp: 350°
yield: 12

Midsummer Night

Midsummer Night is the shortest night of the year (although Lammas may be the warmest), and the fairies come out, as in Shakespeare's <u>Midsummer Night's Dream</u>. Of course, there isn't always a full moon over the revels, but it is a popular night to stay up for as much of the night as possible, and if these treats are pierced and hung up on ribbons (especially interspersed with paper lanterns) they make a combination decoration and snack. What's left can be left for the birds, or people can write wishes on them and hang them up as offerings to the fairy queen.

Gigania's Lunettas

These require no oven at all, only a pizzelle iron and the love required to stand at the stove making each lunetta individually. Luckily, they are quick cooking, taking about 15 minutes for the batch.

> $7/8$ cup sugar
> 3 cups flour
> ½ cup butter
> 3 eggs
> 1 tbsp. lemon extract
> 1 tbsp. orange extract

Pre-heat the pizzelle iron, turning so both sides are hot (if it's not an electric iron), and lightly butter it. Usually that's only needed for the first cookie, and occasionally during the batch if one starts to stick. Always clean off all stuck-on bits before going to the next cookie. Put a tablespoon of batter in the center of the iron and close. Cook 10 seconds to a side. If it is done, it should peel off easily. Lay flat, and add the next tablespoon of batter. Do expect to lose a few to tearing and crumbling.

time: 10 seconds per side
yield: 3 dozen

ASCLEPIUS

Snakes are generally considered a bit spooky by humans. Maybe it's the way they can move without feet. They also descend underground, where they may communicate with the dead. In many cultures serpents are synonymous with wisdom. If a snake licks your ears, you are supposed to be able to understand the speech of animals. The ancient Greeks often had pet snakes who lived in the house, and who were fed milk with special bowls made with places for the snakes to rest while they drank. Demeter's chariot was drawn by a winged snake. Asclepius was supposed to have learned medicine from watching snakes, and his the staff of Asclepius is a staff with one snake wrapped around it. Our modern Caduceus, usually confused with it, used has two snakes and wings on top. The Caduceus was Mercury's staff, and is actually associated with alchemy.

LAMMAS SERPENTS

    1 cup powdered sugar
    1 cup butter
    1 egg
    2½ cup flour
    pinch salt
    1 tsp. vanilla
    ½ tsp. peppermint extract
    or 4 drops peppermint oil
    or 1½ tbsp. creme de menthe

Mix all the ingredients together, cut the dough in two and dye one green and one gold with food coloring (or whatever colors you like) Divide each into 16 pieces and roll them into snake shapes. You can make them more decorative by coiling one around another. Flatten the blunter end, break a peppermint candy with a hammer, and use the chips for eyes (or use nonpareils). You can also roll two colors together to make a striped snake. You may wish to break each of those in two so it will be the same size as the others. Position them on an ungreased cookie sheet in coils, circles, meanders and figure eights. Bake.

time: 8-10 minutes
temp: 375 °
yield: 32

LUGH

Lugh (or Llew) was a Celtic deity, the Lord of many gifts: warrior, healer, sailor, magician, smith, scholar, craftsman. He is known as a god of light, protection, craftsmen, and justice. His feast is Lughnassa, Lughnasadh, or Lammas, celebrated on the first of August.

His grandfather Balor, the lord of the Underworld, was the leader of the Fomorii, a race of old and violent beings. A prophesy said that he would be killed by his grandson, so he tried to have Lugh killed, but Lugh survived and was raised in secret by Mannanan the god of the sea. When he became an adult, he rejoined the Tuatha De Dannan, the people of the Goddess Danu. His great deed was killing Balor by striking out his eye, which killed whoever he looked upon.

LAMMAS CRESCENTS

- ¾ cup powdered sugar
- 1 cup butter
- 1 egg yolk
- 2 tbsp. orange juice
- 1½ tsp. vanilla
- ½ cup ground blanched almonds
- 2¼ cup flour
- ¾ tsp. baking powder
- ¼ tsp. salt
- 2 tsp. fresh orange zest

Mix ingredients together well. Chill in the freezer for at least 15 minutes. Form dough into 2½" crescents on ungreased cookie sheets. Sprinkle with powdered sugar when they come out.

time: 15 minutes
temp: 350°
yield: 2 dozen

Mabon

Mabon, Son of Modron, was a god bearing a name that meant Son, Son of the Mother. His only tale is of being stolen from his mother when three days old, and imprisoned until he was an adult. Not much more is known of the Celtic story, although parts of it evolved into the Arthurian mythos. Mabon has become the name of the fall festival, also called Harvest Home, celebrated around the Autumn Equinox (or in agrarian cultures whenever the harvest is in, which will vary from year to year).

The symbols of Mabon are fall and harvest symbols: the Cornucopia, apples, sheaves of grain, corn dollies, grapes and wine, fall leaves, corn, beans and squash, and all sorts of fruit, nuts, and seeds symbolizing the joy that people have knowing that they will make it through the next winter.

Mabon Leaf Cookies

⅓ cup sugar
5 tbsp. butter
1 egg

⅞ cup cake flour
6 tbsp. ground almonds
¼ tsp. almond extract

Cream wet ingredients until fluffy, then mix in the dry ingredients. This will be a stiff batter, not a dough. Spread through the leaf stencil on greased and floured or lined baking sheets. (The stencils can be obtained from Sweet Celebrations.) Bake. These can be decorated by spreading with melted chocolate and veins scored in, or piping or painting on veins with chocolate.

time: 10 minutes
temp 350°
yield: 40 large or 80 small

Samhain

Samhain (pronounced sow-in) is the old Celtic (pronounced Kel-tik) name for Halloween. This is the beginning of the Celtic Year (the Celts also start the day at nightfall the preceding night). At this time of year the barrier between the visible and invisible world is supposed to be thinner, thus making it easier to communicate with the spirits of the ancestors. It is the last harvest, the time of slaughter, when rural folk "harvest" the meat of the animals that they can't afford to feed through the winter, and start hunting for meat.

There are many ways of describing the change of the seasons: that the Maiden and Mother are gone and the Crone rules; that the Oak King has been replaced by the Holly King; that the Lady sleeps and the Lord rules. As with Beltane and other quarter festivals, bonfires were a part of the ancient celebration of Samhain.

Tiny Samhain Stars

1½ cup sugar
¾ cup butter
1 egg
2 tbsp. molasses

4 cups flour
1 tsp. allspice
½ tsp. cinnamon
¼ tsp. salt

1 cup ground almonds soaking in ¼ cup milk
A beaten egg white and colored sugars

Cream together the sugar and butter, then mix in the egg and molasses. Sift together the dry ingredients and then mix into the sugar/butter mixture, then add the almonds in milk. Chill the dough. Roll 1/8" thick and cut into stars with your smallest star cutter, 1¼" is perfect. Brush with or dip in egg white. Dip in colored sugars - I think at least two colors, orange and black, are good if you can find them. If not, red and gold make a good contrast. It looks neat if you do some of the stars half one color and half the other. (You can make these for any holiday by just choosing appropriate colored sugars.) Bake, on a parchment-covered pan, because the sugar does mess up the pan a lot.

time: 5 minutes
temp: 375°
yield: hundreds

The Winter Lord

The Ancient Celts sometimes described the changing seasons as a contest between the Summer Lord and the Winter Lord for the favors of the Earth Goddess. The Lord of Summer wins at Beltane, but Winter wins at Samhain. In Brittany there are cakes in the shape of antlers called *kornigou* baked for Samhain, to celebrate the god of winter shedding his antlers as he returns to his kingdom.

Divination is another Samhain tradition. One is to bring each person blindfolded to a table on which are saucers containing ashes for sorrow, water for travel, coins for wealth, beans for poverty, etc. What you touch predicts your coming year.

Stags' Antlers

¾ cup sugar
½ cup butter
2 egg yolks
1 egg
¼ cup milk

2¼ cup flour
½ cup cornstarch
½ tsp. soda
½ tsp. cardamom
¼ tsp. salt

Mix the ingredients, chill, form into 1x2" strips. Using scissors, snip two or three nicks out of each strip, which creates prongs on the antler when you curl the dough stick the other direction. Bake on ungreased pans.

time: 10-12 minutes
temp: 350°
yield: 72

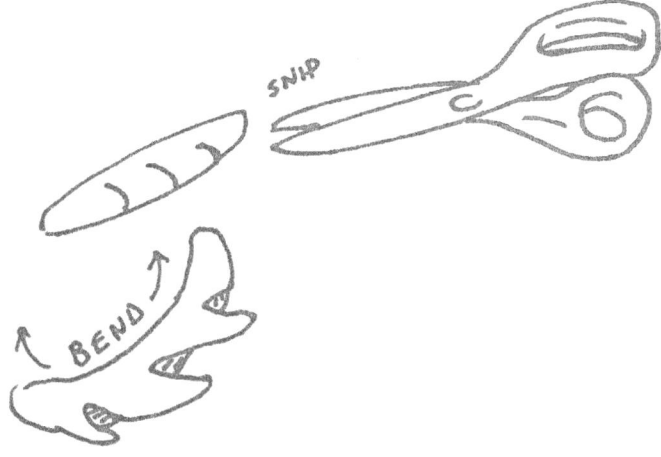

The Crone

The Crone is one of the three faces of the Wiccan Great Goddess: Maiden, Mother and Crone. The Crone carries wisdom and power; she rules over winter, and old age and death. Without the Crone and decay, there would be no recycling and renewal. She breaks down that which is past, and teaches patience, and looking beyond the surface. There are many stories of heroes being challenged to kiss an old, ugly woman, only to discover that when they have, she is in fact a beautiful young woman.

The Triquetra is a symbol of the triple goddess made of three interlocked arcs, and sometimes a circle also interlaced, reinforcing the three in one symbolism.

Crone Cakes

1 cup sugar
1 cup + 2 tbsp. butter
½ cup molasses
2 eggs
½ cup chopped almonds
½ tsp. ground cloves
½ tsp. ground ginger
1/3 cup chopped candied lemon peel
8 ounces marzipan (optional)

4 cup flour
1 tsp. baking powder
¼ tsp. baking soda
2 tsp. cinnamon

Heat together butter, sugar and molasses, cool. Add the other ingredients (except marzipan) and knead together. Divide dough in four pieces and form into 8" long logs, and chill overnight. Slice very thin and bake for a less sweet cookie.

For a sweeter version you can roll out marzipan (dust the board and rolling pin with powdered sugar) and cut out 1" rounds, then sandwich these between the dough slice. If you can find or make a stamp with the triquetra, stamp the cookies before baking.

time: 5 minutes
temp: 400 °
yield: ~250

or if filled
time: 10 minutes
temp: 350°
yield: ~125

Yule

The Winter Solstice, celebrated as Yule, is the longest night, and shortest day of the year. It is associated with the Divine King, or Child of Promise, who is born at Midwinter each year to the Great Mother. At Yule, we honor the Wheel of the Year, a reminder that the although the cold season comes, just as surely it passes again. In the days before artificial light, having less light each day was frighteningly evident, even in parts of the world where they didn't have dangerous cold. Many cultures had traditions with feasting and light and presents and joking where social positions were reversed, giving a needed outlet for the stress of the dark time. The four fire festivals Imbolc, Beltane, Lammas, and Samhain, as well as the solstices and equinoxes, formed the spokes of the Wheel of the Year.

Yule Wheels

- ½ cup powdered sugar
- 1 cup butter
- 2 raw egg yolks
- 2 hard cooked yolks, sieved
- 2½ cups flour
- ¼ tsp. lemon extract
- ¼ tsp. orange extract

Separate two eggs and set the whites aside. Poach the yolks and when cool, press them through a sieve. Mix the sugar and butter together, add the flour, then the hard cooked eggs, then the egg yolks and extracts. Chill the dough, roll into pencil size, and form into rings (optionally you can add crosses). Brush with whisked egg white, and dust with crushed sugar cubes.

time: 12-15 minutes
temp: 350°
yield: 5 dozen

Imbolc

Imbolc is a holiday with many names. It is called Imbolc, meaning "in the belly", as many farm animals are pregnant at this time. It is called Oimelc, meaning "ewe's milk", because sheep give birth around this season. It is called Candlemas, as it is the Festival of Lights. The Celts called it Brigid's Day, as it is also sacred to Brigid, the Celtic Lady of smiths and Inspiration. Modern Heathens call it Disting, after an ancient February fair honoring the Disir (the ancestral mothers). Many celebrate Imbolc, Ostara, and Beltane as different levels of the coming of Spring (as Lammas, Mabon and Samhain are all harvest festivals). Imbolc is the earliest, anticipating its coming. This was the time when plowing started in much of Europe.

Imbolc Bites

The chocolate in these cookies represents the earth in which the seeds holding new life. The sleeping seeds are represented by the pistachios, under the snow, which is represented by the powdered sugar.

- ½ cup sugar
- ¾ cup butter
- 1 egg yolk
- ½ cup chopped pistachios
- 1½ cup flour
- ¼ cup cocoa powder
- 1 tsp. almond extract

Mix the dough thoroughly and chill for at least 15 minutes in the freezer. Form it into balls about the size of a walnut. Bake on ungreased cookie sheets. Dust with powdered sugar.

time: 7-9 minutes
temp: 375°
yield: 3 dozen

Ostara

The first day of spring (the spring equinox) is celebrated as Ostara or Eostre. Ostara is named by the Venerable Bede as the name of a goddess to whom the pagans offered cakes in the spring, but little else is known of her. Ostara gave her name to the Christian spring holiday Easter, along with the traditions of the Easter Rabbit (or Hare in Europe) and Easter eggs. Where ever you live, it is natural to wish to start celebrating when spring arrives: days finally get longer than nights, birds start laying eggs, seeds start sprouting.

Rabbit Ears

These are fried cookies, well known in Norway as Fattigman Bakkels (Poorman's Cookies), but there are similar variants in most cultures.

> 1/3 cup powdered sugar
> ¼ cup whipping cream
> 2 whole eggs (or 4 yolks)
> 2 cups flour
> ½ tsp. cardamom
> lard or oil for frying

I actually don't measure these. I make a pile of flour on the rolling board, make a well in it and crack in a couple of eggs, knead them in, and moisten with cream until it kneads well. Toss on powdered sugar and spice until it is "sweet enough". If you are measuring, you can make it richer by using only yolks. Mix and knead, roll as thin as you can. Using a sharp knife or pizza cutter, cut into diamond shapes. Cut a slit in the center of each and pull one end through slit to make twists. Deep-fat fry four or five at a time, and drain on brown paper. Sprinkle with confectioner's sugar or cinnamon sugar.

time: 20 minutes per batch,
less than one minute per Rabbit Ear.
oil temp: 365°
yield: 4 dozen

Lakshmi

Lakshmi is the Goddess of good luck, beauty and wealth, and the wife of Vishnu. She is pictured as a beautiful woman with a golden complexion, wearing gold-embroidered red clothing. She is often shown standing or sitting on a lotus flower and holding lotus buds, with gold coins pouring from her hands. She is addressed as Mata (mother) rather than Diva (goddess). She is also called Shri, the female energy of the Supreme Being.

These cookies require a mold of some sort to imprint the design on top. You can make it yourself, or use an existing design. Flowers would be appropriate for Lakshmi, or a peacock or moon or elves. If you wish to hang them as decorations, pierce each cookie with a small straw or skewer before baking.

Sandalwood Print Cookies

2 eggs
2 cups sugar
¼ warm red wine
1 tbsp. lemon juice
¼ tsp. ground cloves
½ tsp. fresh ground nutmeg
1 tbsp. Saunders (ground sandalwood)
   OR red food coloring

scant 3 cups flour
1 tsp. baking powder
fresh lemon zest
pinch of salt

Beat the eggs and sugar together until stiff. Sift the dry ingredients together. Gently fold the flour into the eggs, and add the wine, juice and food coloring (if you can't find sandalwood). Knead until smooth and soft but not sticky; add more flour if needed. Let rest at room temperature for an hour. Roll ¼" thick, and press dough into molds dusted with cornstarch. Separate and trim edges of cookies with knife or pizza wheel. Leave out to dry for 5-24 hours. This keeps the design when the cookies rise. It helps if you wedge a wooden spoon in the oven door while baking to keep it slightly open. You may decorate them with gold petal dust.

time: 25 minutes
temp: 300°
yield: 4 dozen

Ganesha

Ganesha is the Hindu god of wisdom, and destroyer of vanity. Remover of Obstacles. I am fond of this rather modernized version of the story of why he has an elephant's head. Once when Shiva was out, Parvati was lonely, so she made a boy and told him to guard the bathroom. When her husband came back, he found Ganesha denying him entrance to his own bath, and not recognizing the boy, cut off his head. His mother was quite annoyed when she discovered this and required her lord to fix the problem ASAP. So he sent a servant out to get him a head. The first animal the servant found was an Elephant, so he cut off it's head and brought it back. Shiva put the head on the boy's body and brought him back to life, but his mother was not amused. "Everyone is going to make fun of him with that head!" she complained.

So Ganesh was made the intermediary, the god of "red tape", and all prayers must go to him first, before calling on any other god. He has also always retained his childlike fondness for sweets. He wrote the Upanishads with the end of his tusk, and rides on a large rat.

Ganesha's Treats

You may recognize these as Snickerdoodles. We've found Ganesha to be very fond of them.

    1 ¼ cup sugar
    1 cup butter
    2 eggs
    ½ tsp. vanilla
    $2^2/_3$ cups flour
    1 tbsp. cream tartar
    1 tsp. baking soda

Mix, chill (this is a really sticky dough, so you must chill it). Spread cinnamon sugar on a plate:

    ½ cup sugar
    2 tbsp. ground cinnamon

Roll 1" balls in the sugar. Bake (do not over bake).

time: 10-13 minutes
temp: 400°
yield: 4 dozen

Kali

Kali is associated in western fiction as a death goddess, patron of the Thuggee murder cult. While this is a small part of the truth, Kali is more accurately seen as the protective and destructive form of the Great Mother, the ferocious form of the warrior Goddess Durga and the mother goddess Parvati. The common image of her standing on Shiva is from a legend where she was out of control in battle rage, and Shiva flung himself under her feet, which shocked her (hence the protruding tongue), and ended her homicidal rage. She wears skulls and corpses as jewelry, but she is the form the goddess takes when violence is necessary. Her necklace of 50 skulls stands for the letters of the Sanskrit alphabet, and symbolizes knowledge. Her three eyes see the past, present and future, and her name means Time.

Kali's Skulls

1½ cup sugar	3-3½ cups flour
¾ cup butter	2 tsp. baking powder
½ cup white corn syrup	½ tsp. soda
2 tbsp. milk	½ tsp. cardamom
½ tsp. anise extract	½ tsp. nutmeg
½ tsp. cloves	½ tsp. mace
½ tsp. ginger	1 tsp. cinnamon

Mix all ingredients and let ripen for 1-7 days, then roll them out and cut as small as you can. If you can find tiny skull-shaped cutters or stamps, great. If not, roll them into rods smaller than pencils and break them off into ½" pieces, give them a last roll, pressing to make the center thinner than the ends, and call them bones. (This is a good recipe for kids to help make.) Or you can simply not worry about what they look like and make them as small as you can, whether by pinching, cutting, rolling or whatever, and bake. (The original recipe was not Hindu and called for lard, which is fine, but that would be inappropriate for Kali.)

time: 8 minutes
temp: 350°
yield: ½ gallon

Kuan-Yin

Healing goddess Kuan-yin is known as the compassionate one, the goddess of mercy. When offered a chance to live in heaven with the other gods and goddesses, she declined, refusing to leave humans as long as they were suffering, choosing instead to stay on earth to offer them her aid, especially to mothers and young children. She is known by many names throughout Asia - Quan Yin, Quan'am, Kanin, and Kannon. She is shown holding pearls of illumination and pouring forth the water of life, or rice, for fertility and sustenance.

Kuan-Yin Bars

Crust:
- ½ cup butter
- ¼ cup brown sugar
- ½ cup whole wheat pastry flour
- ¼ cup wheat germ
- ¼ cup white flour

Apricot filling:
- $2/3$ dried chopped apricots
- 2 eggs
- ½ sugar
- 1 tbsp. molasses
- ¼ honey
- $1/3$ cup flour
- $1/3$ cup flour
- ½ tsp baking powder
- ½ tsp. vanilla
- ½ cup chopped walnuts

Cream together the butter and sugar, then add the flours. This makes a crumbly crust. Pat it into a 8x8 square pan, and bake for 20 minutes. While the crust bakes, simmer the cover the apricots with water, simmer for 10 minutes, cool and chop well. Mix eggs and other filling ingredients, adding apricots last. Spread the filling over the crust and bake for another 30 minutes. Cut into bars after cooling.

time: 20 + 30 = 50 minutes
temp: 350°
yield: 12

Amaterasu

Amaterasu is the Japanese Goddess of sun and rice. She was a great weaver, but her brother Susanoo, god of Storms, was jealous of her popularity. He killed a horse and threw it into her weaving room, ruining and wrecking everything. She became depressed and hid in a cave, making endless night on earth. No one could lure her out until Uzume, goddess of mirth, rolled a large mirror in front of the cave, then started dancing on an overturned tub. Amaterasu came out to hear what the laughter and drumming was about, and saw her reflection in the mirror. While she was dazzled, they blocked the entrance to the cave so she could not go back in.

Amaterasu Rice Cookies

¼ cup honey
2 Tbsp. butter
1 egg
1 tsp vanilla
1 cup white rice flour
1 cup nuts (ground)
¼ cup golden raisins
¼ cup apricots
¼ cup nuts

Mix, chill overnight. Blend the dried fruit and nuts together, moistening, if needed, with a few drops of water. Roll dough into 1" balls with a dab of the fruit in the middle. Place on cookie sheet and flatten slightly. Bake on lined cookie sheets.

time: 15 minutes
temp. 350°
yield: 2 dozen

 PELE

Pele is the Hawaiian goddess of volcanoes. She can take the form of lava, or of a white dog, or of a beautiful woman.

There is a story of her as a skilled rider of the holua. The holua seems to be something like surfing, but on land on steep stone ramps. Once the chief Papalauahi invited Pele to join them in a holua contest. Papalauahi was the winner, and Pele sent a flood of lava which overran the chiefs, turning them to lava pillars, which can still be seen in lower Puna.

PELE SHORTBREAD

½ cup dark brown sugar
1 ¼ cups whole wheat flour
3 tablespoons rolled oats
½ tsp. cream of tartar
¼ tsp. baking soda
½ cup butter
1 ½ tsp. ginger
¼ tsp. allspice

Process 3 tablespoons rolled oats in a blender and blend with the flour. Rub flours in the butter, then blend in the sugar and spices. Press crumbly dough into pan. Score for breaking apart after baking. Sprinkle with red and yellow sugar. Bake.

time: 25-20 minutes
temp: 350°
yield: 16 large or 64 small

COYOTE

In many Native American stories, the Earth and Sky are formed by two brothers. Eagle or Wolf generally want the world to be more pleasant, and Coyote wants to make things, shall we say, "more interesting". One story tells that women once put their baskets outside the door at night, which would be filled with food in the morning. Coyote thought this would lead women to be lazy, so he decided that they should now work to fill them.

Another story tells of how Coyote stole fire from the Fire people to bring to his own folk by making a wig of reeds and letting them light up while dancing around their fire, then running back home with it. In many of these stories Coyote suffers more than others from his tricks. Men admired his cleverness, but even though he was often causing trouble, he was also most often the one who suffered from it.

COYOTE SNACKS

2 cups water
5 heaping tsp. star anise
2 cups brown sugar
1 tsp. vanilla
6 cup flour
2 tsp. baking soda
1 cup butter

Make syrup by bring to boil 2 cups water, add star anise, and boil 15 minutes. Then add the brown sugar and boil for 10 more minutes. Stir in the vanilla. Cut together the flour, baking soda and butter. Mix the syrup into the flour mixture, knead well. Chill, roll lumps of dough into pencil-sized ropes, and cut into ¼" pieces. (They cut more easily if you chill them in the freezer for 15 minutes before cutting.) Spread evenly on an ungreased cookie sheet, bake.

This dough can also be rolled out and cut out into shapes with small cookie cutters. I like rabbits, but as small lumps, they are like the corn Coyote was often stealing, and you can throw them up in the air and catch them in your mouth better than flat cookies.

time: 6-7 minutes
temp: 375°
yield: ½ gallon

WHITE BUFFALO CALF WOMAN

White Buffalo Calf Woman appeared to the Lakota Nation two thousand years ago, at a time when the people were starving because there was no game, and brought them a sacred pipe. She taught them about the buffalo, as well as the seven sacred ceremonies: the sweat lodge, the child naming, the healing ceremony, the adoption ceremony, the marriage ceremony, the vision quest, and the Sun Dance. When she left, White Buffalo Calf Woman told them that she would return someday. She then turned back into a white, then red, then yellow, then black buffalo before she disappeared.

There is a prophesy that in the time of the White Buffalo the red, white, yellow and black people would be united. In 1994 a white buffalo calf was born named Miracle in North Dakota, and two more have been born since, and many modern people think that the White Buffalo time is now.

WHITE BUFFALO CALF WOMAN CHIPS

(although little boys may call them Buffalo Chips)

    $1/3$ cup wild rice
    (or chopped pecans)
    1 cup sugar
    ½ cup butter
    1 egg
    2 tbsp. cocoa flour
    1 bag white chocolate chips
    1 cup corn meal
    1 cup rice flour
    ¼ cup tapioca flour

Boil the rice for 30 minutes and drain well. Mix all ingredients together, drop onto parchment or well-greased pans, and bake. The rice and corn meal give it an unusual texture.

time: 17 minutes
temp: 350°
yield: 3 dozen

MANITOU

Manitou is a term for Deity which means "Great Spirit". Manitou is the creator and protector of mankind, which the Christian missionaries equated with Jehovah. Another term for the Great Spirit is Wakan Tanka.

The Haudenosaune (Iroquois) called it Orenda Power. The Inuit called it Sila. Manitou is a Huron (Algonquin) name for the Creator.

I found some interesting stories connecting the Anasazi people with the lost tribes of Israel. The Anasazi describe themselves as the chosen people of Manitou, although their name literally means "ancient enemies". (Of course, many tribes are now burdened with the names given them by their enemies, who identified them to European translators.)

If you don't have a maple leaf cookie cutter, you can use a circle and score a cross across each cookie. The quartered cross is a Manitou symbol.

MANITOUS

These are also called maple sables.

2 egg yolks
1 cup butter
1¼ cups maple sugar
(or ¾ cup maple sugar and ½ cup white sugar)
1⅞ cups flour
2 tsp. vanilla
¼ cup walnuts

Blend the maple sugar with butter. Process ¼ cup walnuts in a blender with sugar, and beat it in. Add the other ingredients, and chill 2-3 hours. Roll dough 1/8", cut with maple leaf-shaped cookie cutters (you can score veins with a toothpick or a stamp), and bake. Make the creme filling, and sandwich between cookies.

Crème filling:

¼ cup sugar
¼ cup ground walnuts
2 egg yolks
¾ cup butter
3 tbsp. maple syrup

Process the walnuts and sugar in a blender and cream with butter. Beat egg yolks until lemony. Heat the maple syrup to a boil (in the microwave that's easy) and gradually beat it into the egg yolks. Cool completely and blend in the butter mixture.

time: 8-10 minutes
temp: 350°
yield: 2 dozen

Corbie

The Raven and Crow were revered in many cultures. They are known for their intelligence, having been taught to speak, and as carrion eaters, which has caused them to be associated with battles, because they and the wolves are the ones who "clean up" after them. The Crow is a huge bird, and the Raven even larger. Corbie is an English nickname for either of these black birds. Their intelligence is well know- Aesop told of a thirsty crow finding a pitcher of water in which the water level was too low for her to reach with her beak, but she dropped pebbles into it until the water finally reached a level where she could drink.

Corbie's Bribes

>	1 cup sugar
>	¾ cup butter
>	2 eggs
>	½ cup molasses
>	2 cups flour
>	2½ teaspoons baking soda
>	1 tsp. cinnamon
>	1½ teaspoon ginger

This is a gingersnap recipe. Mix all the ingredients together thoroughly, until dough is smooth and creamy. These are drop cookies. Spoon 12 to a greased or lined cookie sheet, and bake.

Time: 10 minutes
temp. 350°
yield: 3 dozen

CHAC

Chac is the Mayan god of rain. He is a benevolent god who, when he heard his devotees' prayers, responded by sending his copious tears down to earth as rain. He took the form of a serpent when it pleased him. He was also considered to be divided into four equal entities who represented the four winds. Kukulan was the name of the wind god. His likeness can be found carved on temple walls in southern Mexico and Guatemala.

Chac Mocha Snakes

2 egg whites
½ cup superfine sugar
¼ tsp. cream of tartar
1 tsp. espresso coffee powder
¼ tsp. ground cinnamon
1 tbsp cocoa powder
chocolate chips

First dissolve the espresso coffee powder in a teaspoon of boiling water. Mix the cocoa powder and cinnamon into the sugar. Make the meringue by beating egg whites and cream of tartar until it forms stiff peaks, then gradually beat in the sugar and cinnamon. Fold in the dissolved coffee. Put the meringue in a pastry bag, and pipe into snake shapes. You can practice on waxed paper until you have the hang of it, then put it back into the bag, and pipe onto parchment or brown paper bags. Add eyes with miniature chocolate chips. Bake.

time: 1 hour
temp: 200°
yield: 5-6 dozen

Baba Yaga

Baba Yaga was a witch who appeared in many Russian fairy tales. She traveled, not by broomstick, but in a flying mortar, guiding it with the pestle. She often helped the young heroes and heroines of the tales, but they had to be brave. She showed no hesitation in eating or otherwise ingeniously punishing the evil sisters and brothers in the stories who were not brave, hardworking, and virtuous. Her house stood on chicken legs, constantly turning in all directions, and the fence around her yard had skulls with burning eyes on each post.

Baba Yagas

    1 cup powdered sugar
    2 cups (one pound) butter
    1 cup chopped walnuts
    4½ cups flour
    1 tbsp. vanilla

Chop the walnuts fairly finely, but not ground. Mix all the ingredients together. Roll into balls about one inch in diameter. Bake until bottoms just barely start to brown. Have ready a pan with a pound of powdered sugar in it, and roll the balls in the powdered sugar as soon as they come out hot from oven. Be careful! I often singe my fingers, but if you use a spoon, you are liable to break the balls open and fill the powdered sugar with crumbs. They are even more fragile than usual when hot.

My mother made them bigger than this, but I am a natural slob and find a slightly smaller ball can go right in your mouth without biting, which reduces the mess. So make them a bit smaller than your mouth, because they gain diameter in the sugar. These will keep for months - if surrounded by flaming skulls, and in a tin.

time: 7 minutes
temp: 350°
yield: 1 gross

Strega Nona

Strega Nona means "Grandmother Witch". The Stregae are a special kind of magic-workers from Italy. Even modern Italian villages sometimes have a woman who can help love-smitten youngsters, or older folk with illnesses that doctors can't help, or who can help turn away bad luck if it has attached itself to someone.

Although I have met real Stregae since, I first heard of them in Tommy de Paola's books about Strega Nona. One of his stories is a variation on the old "sorcerer's apprentice" tale waning of the dangers of fooling with magick, and to never start anything you don't know how to stop! In this case, Strega Nona's helper starts her cauldron making pasta and can't remember the magical word to make the pasta stop. This creates an avalanche of pasta until Strega Nona comes back to turn it off.

Strega Nonas

²/₃ cups sugar
1 egg white
1 tsp. freshly grated lemon peel
½ to 1 tsp. fresh lemon juice
1 cup pine nuts (pignoli)
7-8 oz. almond paste

Line a cookie sheet with foil and lightly oil it. Separate two eggs, and whisk lightly. Break or chop the tube of almond paste into small pieces, then beat the egg whites and sugar into it until smooth. A powerful mixer makes this much easier. Mix in 1 teaspoon of freshly grated lemon peel and juice, just enough juice to make it feel really sticky. Keep your fingers coated with sugar to keep the dough from sticking to you too badly. Chill, and divide into 32 pieces. Roll them into balls, and roll each ball in the pine nuts. I then roll the lumpy balls back and forth a little so that the pine nuts will stick into the dough well and not fall out after baking. Bake on the foiled sheet in a moderate oven, and take out when they begin to brown just a bit on the bottom. These will last 2 weeks if kept in a tin.

time: 22-25 minutes
temp: 325°
yield: 32

Witches' Hats

The pointy hat of the witch has its roots in the same pointy-hat-with-a-veil of the medieval princess. Country women would wear these hats, but added large brims to keep the sun out. A generation later, when fashionable ladies had turned to the (even sillier) hats that looked like they were wearing little jeweled doghouses on their heads, they made fun of country women who were so unfashionable that they wore a style a generation out of date. People have often mocked what made them nervous by dressing them in outmoded fashions. Since they started making picture storybooks in the 16th century, those images have stayed with us.

Witches' Hats

With purchased ingredients these become a "no bake" cookie for kids.

>chocolate wafers
>chocolate kisses
>1 tube decorator frosting
>(or leftover home-made icing)

Using a dab of icing, stick an unwrapped chocolate kiss in the center of a wafer, then pipe a decorative band around the bottom of the "hat". With another color of frosting you can add a buckle. Simple. Or make your own chocolate wafers, and they can be any size you want. Larger hats can be topped with chocolate waffle cones, which look much more like hats. For smaller hats you can use chocolate chips.

>1 cup butter
>1 cup sugar
>1 egg
>1 tsp. vanilla, almond or peppermint extract
>2½ cups flour
>½ cup cocoa powder
>½ tsp. baking powder

Mix, roll into 2 logs and chill, slice thin, and bake on parchment or lightly oiled paper. If the chocolate tops are set on while the cookies are still hot, the bottoms will melt and stick on.

time: 6 minutes
temp: 350°
yield: 3-4 dozen

Magic Wands

Magic workers all over the world have used wands to direct the energy they are moving to where they want it. Wood is a popular choice for wands because, after all, it is the nature and function of wood is to draw up the nutrients and water through the tree to the leaves, and it moves energy the same way. A wizard sometimes carries a staff, which is basically a large wand. It could also double as a walking stick or a weapon, but is harder to conceal. It has been suggested that brooms or pitchforks were ways of concealing staffs.

Modern wands are made from anything from a natural stick found under a tree to wands composed of many materials. Optical quartz rod, created for fiber optics, has been found to be a wonderful conductor, as are more traditional silver or copper metal wands. Many wands also incorporate crystals, taking advantages of their properties.

These wands, however, are simply good to eat.

Magic Wands

1 cup sugar
1 cup butter
1 egg
1 pat butter
2¼ cups flour
1 tsp. baking powder
1 tsp. grated orange peel
4 oz. semisweet chocolate
gold or silver dragees or colored sugar

These are a spritz cookie- formed by forcing the dough through a cookie gun or press. Cream the sugar, butter and egg together. Mix in the flour, baking powder and orange peel (fresh is best). Use the small star tip, and press out sticks- about finger long. If you try longer wands, they will probably break. Bake on lightly greased sheets. When cool, gently melt chocolate and butter. It's easiest in a microwave. Dip one end of each cookie in chocolate and then in the dragees. (The dragees look pretty, but adults will prefer fewer as they are hard, and the cookies tender. Alternately, you can add 3 tbsp. cocoa powder to the dough and dip the tips in white chocolate and colored sugar instead of dragees.)

time: 10-12 minutes
temp: 350°
yield: 4 dozen

INDEX

Amalthea 75
Amalthea's Horns 76
Amaterasu 135
Amaterasu's Rice Balls 136
Anansi 13
Anansi Cookies 14
Arianrhod 91
Artemis 69
Asclepius 109
Athena 73
Athena's Owls 74
Attis 9
Attis Cookies 10
Aphrodite 65
Aphrodite's Doves 66
Baba Yaga 149
Baba Yagas 150
Bastet 47
Bastets 48
Bean Tighe 81
Bean Tighe Stars 82
Beltane 99, 121, 123
Beltane Flowers 100
Bes 57
Bes Cookies 58
Blodeuwedd 91, 93
Blodeuwedd's Flowers 94
Bows of Artemis 70
Breasts of Ishtar 8
Brigit 83
Brigit's Crosses 84
Caduceus 59
Cerridwen 91

Chac 147
Chac's Mocha Snacks 148
Cookie Cutter Websites........................... 2
Corbie's Bribes..................................... 146
Coyote 139
Coyote Snacks..................................... 140
Crone 119
Crone Cakes.. 120
Crow.. 145
Cybele 9
Dagda 83, 85, 87
Dagda's Clubs 86
Death by Chocolate Brownies 88
Demeter 67, 71
Donis... 3-4
Epona 95
Epona's Horses 96
Fenris 15, 29, 31
Fenris Bars.. 30
Frey 19, 33, 35, 39
Frey's Cakes... 36
Freya 15, 21, 33, 35, 39
Freya's Cookies.................................... 34
Frigga 25
Frigga's Handmaidens........................ 26
Gaea 79
Gaeas 80
Ganesha... 129
Ganesha's Treats 130
Gluten-Free Gourmet Flour 2
Great Mother 3
Green Man 97, 101, 103
Green Man Nut Balls 102
Hecate 71
Hecate's Moons.................................... 72

Herne 97
Herne's Beasts 98
Hathor 49, 55
Hathor's Sistra 56
Hel 15, 17
Hel's Thumbprints 18
Hermes 59
Hermes Coins 60
Horned God 97
Imbolc 121, 123
Imbolc Bites 124
Inanna 5
Inanna's Stars 6
Ishtar 5, 7
Isis 51, 53
Isis Cakes 52
Janus 61
Janus Cookies 62
Kali 131
Kali's Skulls 132
Kores 68
Kuan-Yin 133
Kuan-Yin Bars 134
Labrys Cookies 78
Lakshmi 127
Lammas 111, 121, 123
Lammas Crescents 112
Lammas Serpents 110
Litha 105, 107
Litha Shells 106
Loki 15, 17, 21, 25, 39, 43
Lokis 16
Lugh 111
Lughnasadh 111
Mabon 113, 123

Mabon Leaf Cookies 114
Madelines 105
Magic Wands 155-156
Manitou 143
Manitous.. 144
Mielikki 45
Mielikki Bars 46
Mimir 27
Mimir's Well Cookies 28
Morrigan 87
Mjolnir... 39
Mjolnirs 40
No-Bake Green Men 104
Norns... 41
Norn Cakes 42
Odin 15, 19, 21, 23, 25, 27, 39
Odin's Shields 20
Osiris 51, 53
Osiris Puzzle Cookie 54
Ostara 123, 125
Pan 63
Pan Pipes 64
Peanutbutter Donis 4
Pele 137
Pele's Shortbread 138
Persephone 67, 71
Pizzelles 108
Potnia 77
Puzzle Cookie 54
Ra... 47, 49, 55
Ra Bars 50
Rabbit Ears 126
Raven 145
Rhiannon 89
Runes 23

Rune Cookies 24
Samhain 115, 121, 123
Sandbakkels 34
Sandalwood Print Cookies 128
Saunders 128
Silver Wheels 92
Skadi 43
Skadi's Skates 44
Sleipnir 21
Sleipnirs 22
Snickerdoodles 130
Springerle 21
Stag's Antlers 118
Strega Nona 151
Strega Nonas 152
Tammuz 7
Tiny Samhain Stars 116
Titania 107-108
Titania's Lunettas 108
Thor 15, 37, 39, 43
Thor's Goats 38
Triquetra 119
Tyr 29, 31
Tyr's Hands 32
Uraeus 47
Wafers of Rhiannon 90
White Buffalo Calf Woman 141
White Buffalo Calf Woman Chips 142
Winter Lord 117
Witches' Hats 153-154
Yemaya 11
Yemaya Cookies 12
Yule 121
YuleWheels 122

Cookies Indexed by Distinctive Ingredients

Almonds: see Crone cakes, Dagda's Clubs, Frey's Cakes, Frigga's Handmaidens, Green Man Nut Balls, Inanna's Stars, Lammas Crescents, Mabon Leaf Cookies, Odin's Shields, Norn Cakes, Rune Cookies, Silver Wheels, Skadi's Skates, Strega Nonas, Tiny Samhain Stars

Apricots: see Amaterasu Rice Balls, Isis Cakes, Kwan-Yin Bars

Anise: see Anansi Cookies, Coyote Snacks, Kali's Skulls, Sleipnirs

Bar Cookies: see Death by Chocolate Brownies, Fenris Bars, Mielikki Bars, Norn Cakes, Pele's Shortbread, Ra Bars.

Chocolate: see Death by Chocolate Brownies, Gaeas, Hathor's Sistra, Imbolc Bites, Magic Wands, Mielikki Bars, Pan Pipes, White Buffalo Woman Chips, Witches' Hats, Yemaya Cookies

Coffee: see Chac's Mocha Snacks

Cookie Cutters: see Athena's Owls, Beltane Flowers, Frigga's Handmaidens, Hecate's Moons, Hermes Coins, Herne's Beasts, Inanna's Stars, Isis Cakes, Kali's Skulls, Labrys Cookies, Manitous, Osiris Puzzle, Thor's Goats, Silver Wheels, Tyr's Hands, Yemaya Cookies

Cookie Stamps: see Athena's Owls, Crone Cakes, Lakshmi's Sandalwood Print Cookies, Mjolnirs, Sleipnirs, Wafers of Rhiannon

Cream Cheese: see Athena's Owls, Inanna's Stars, Mielikki Bars, Mimir's Wells, Yemaya's Cookies

Fried Cookies: see Brigit's Crosses, Rabbit Ears

Ginger: see Corbie's Bribes, Lokis, Pele's Shortbread

Gingersnaps: Corbie's Bribes

Hazelnuts: Hel's Thumb Prints, Dagda's clubs

Icing Recipes: see Anansi's Cookies, Beltane Flowers, Blodwen's Flowers, Green Man Nut Balls, Hathor's Sistra, Hecate's Moons, Hermes Coins, Manitous, Tyr's Hands

Jam Cookies: see Attis Cookies, Bean Tighe Stars, Freya's Cookies, Hel's Thumbprints, Inanna's Stars, Isis Cakes, Mimir's Wells

Lebkuchen: see Odin's Shields, Norn Cakes, Rune Cookies

Lemon: see Beltane Flowers, Bes Cookies, Bows of Artemis, Frigga's Handmaidens, Kores, Lakshmi's Sandalwood Print Cookies, Norn Cakes, Odin's Shields, Thor's Goats, Titania's Lunettas, Ra Bars, Silver Wheels, Sleipnirs, Strega Nonas, Yule Wheels

Maple: see Manitous

Marzipan: see Crone Cakes, Strega Nonas

Meringues: see Aphrodite's Doves, Chac's Serpents, Janus Cookies

Mint: see Bastets, Hathor's Sistra, Lammas Serpents, Mielikki Bars, Yemaya's Cookies

Mocha: see Chac's Mocha Snacks

No-Bake: see No-Bake Green Men, Witches' Hats

No Wheat: see Aphrodite's Doves, Amaterasu Rice Balls, Chac's Mocha Snacks, Janus Cookies, Strega Nonas, White Buffalo Woman Chips, Gluten-Free Gourmet Dough

Orange: see Janus Cookies, Lammas Crescents, Magic Wands, Pan Pipes, Titania's Lunettes

Pecans: see Dagda's Clubs, Death by Chocolate Brownies, Fenris Bars, White Buffalo Calf Woman Chips

Peppernuts: see Coyote Snacks, Kali's Skulls, Mjolnirs, Tyr's Hands

Pine Nuts: see Strega Nonas

Pistachios: see Gaeas, Green Man Nut Balls, Imbolc Bites

Play-Dough-Type: see Bastets, Lammas Serpents, Peanutbutter Donis

DIVINE COOKIES

Poppy Seeds: see Kores

Royal Icing: see Tyr's Hands, Hecate's Moons

Savory Cookies: see Anansi Cookies, Epona's Horses, Labrys Cookies

Sesame Seeds: see Isis Cakes

Shortbread-type: see Frey's Cakes, Baba Yagas, Labrys Cookies, Lammas Serpents, Pele's Shortbread

Sour cream: see Amalthea's Horns, Bows of Artemis

Slice-And-Bake: see Bes Cookies, Crone Cakes, Lokis, Witches' Hats, Yemaya Cookies

Spice Cookies: see Corbie's Bribes, Hecate's Moons, Lokis, Kali's Skulls, Tiny Samhain Stars, Tyr's Hands

Stencil Cookies: see Mabon Leaf Cookies

Walnuts: see Baba Yagas, Breasts of Ishtar, Kuan-Yin bars, Manitous

www.ingramcontent.com/pod-product-compliance
Lightning Source LLC
Chambersburg PA
CBHW032119090426
42743CB00007B/400